GOD'S MASTERWORK

A Concerto in Sixty-Six Movements

Volume Three

Hosea through Malachi

From the Bible-teaching ministry of

CHARLES R. SWINDOLL

INSIGHT FOR LIVING

Chuck graduated in 1963 from Dallas Theological Seminary, where he now serves as the school's fourth president, helping to prepare a new generation of men and women for the ministry. Chuck has served in pastorates in three states: Massachusetts, Texas, and California, including almost twenty-three years at the First Evangelical Free Church in Fullerton, California. His sermon messages have been aired over radio since 1979 as the *Insight for Living* broadcast. A best-selling author, Chuck has written numerous books and booklets on many subjects.

Based on the outlines and transcripts of Chuck's sermons, the study guide text is coauthored by Gary Matlack, a graduate of Texas Tech University and Dallas Theological Seminary. He also wrote the Living Insights sections.

Editor in Chief:
Cynthia Swindoll

Coauthor of Text:
Gary Matlack

Assistant Editor and Writer:
Wendy Peterson

Copy Editors:
Tom Kimber
Deborah Gibbs
Marco Salazar
Glenda Schlahta

Cover Designer:
Nina Paris

Text Designer:
Gary Lett

Graphics System Administrator:
Bob Haskins

Publishing System Specialist:
Alex Pasieka

Director, Communications Division:
John Norton

Marketing Manager:
Alene Cooper

Project Coordinator:
Colette Muse

Production Coordinator:
Don Bernstein

Printer:
Sinclair Printing Company

Unless otherwise identified, all Scripture references are from the New American Standard Bible, © The Lockman Foundation 1960, 1962, 1963, 1968, 1971, 1972, 1973, 1975, 1977, 1995. Used by permission. Scripture taken from the Holy Bible, New International Version © 1973, 1978, 1984 International Bible Society, used by permission of Zondervan Bible Publishers. The other translation cited is the *New King James Version* (NKJV).

Series ISBN 0-8499-1474-4—*God's Masterwork: A Concerto in Sixty-Six Movements*
Study guide ISBN 0-8499-8740-7—*Volume Three: Hosea–Malachi*
COVER PHOTOGRAPHY: Comstock
COVER BACKGROUND PHOTO: Superstock
Printed in the United States of America

CONTENTS

INTRODUCTION

Several years ago I conducted an informal survey—in sort of a "man on the street" fashion—to find out how familiar people were with Habakkuk, one of the twelve minor prophets whose book appears toward the end of the Old Testament. I simply asked, "What does Habakkuk mean to you?" Here are some of the answers I received:

"I think it's a word spelled backwards."

"It's a Jewish holiday."

"Isn't that a disease of the lower back?"

Hilarious! These responses, however, also reveal that most folks don't spend much time in the Minor Prophets. Perhaps that's because their collective name is a bit deceptive. Though their books are minor in size compared to such major prophets as Isaiah, Jeremiah, and Ezekiel, the minor prophets were no less important to the lives of the ancient Jews.

These stern-minded men proclaimed God's displeasure over sin, announced His judgment, offered His mercy and forgiveness, and encouraged His people about the sure future their covenant-keeping God had prepared for them.

Though dead, these prophets still speak today—telling us what matters most to God, revealing His tender care, and urging us to live like true citizens of His kingdom.

So, welcome to the Minor Prophets. Let's listen attentively to these twelve major instruments in the symphony of God's Masterwork.

Chuck Swindoll

Chuck Swindoll

PUTTING TRUTH INTO ACTION

K nowledge apart from application falls short of God's desire for His children. He wants us to apply what we learn so that we will change and grow. This study guide was prepared with these goals in mind. As you go through the following pages, we hope your desire to discover biblical truth will grow as your understanding of God's Word increases and that you will be encouraged to apply what you've learned.

To assist you in your study, we've included a section called Living Insights at the end of each lesson. These exercises will challenge you to study further and to think of specific ways to put your discoveries into action.

There are many ways to use this guide—in personal devotions, group studies, discussions with friends and family, and Sunday school classes. And, of course, it's an ideal study aid when you're listening to its corresponding *Insight for Living* radio series.

To benefit most from this study guide, we would encourage you to consider it a spiritual journal. That's why we've included space in the Living Insights for recording your thoughts and discoveries. We hope you'll return to those sections often for review and encouragement as you continue to grow in your walk with Christ.

Gary Matlack

Gary Matlack
Coauthor of Text
Author of Living Insights

GOD'S MASTERWORK

A Concerto in Sixty-Six Movements

Volume Three

Hosea through Malachi

CHRONOLOGY OF PROPHETS

9th Century Prophets	8th Century Prophets	7th and 6th Century Prophets	Exilic Prophets	Postexilic Prophets
	Jonah Amos Hosea			

Israel

Judah

Obadiah
Joel

Isaiah
Micah

Nahum
Zephaniah
Habakkuk
Jeremiah

Daniel
Ezekiel

Haggai
Zechariah
Malachi

Assyrian Exile of Israel 722 B.C.

Babylonian Exile of Judah 586 B.C.

Chapter 1

HOSEA: LOVE THAT NEVER DIES
A Survey of Hosea

How does God feel when His people are unfaithful?

Hosea knew. His writings, perhaps more than any other author's, give us God's gut-level reaction to the disloyalty of the Israelites. Hosea was well-acquainted with God's heartbreak, not just because he preached and wrote about Israel's rejection of God, but because he lived it out on a personal level.

In order to illustrate the magnitude of Israel's infidelity and the punishment they deserved for it, the Lord commanded Hosea to marry a woman who would leave him to pursue promiscuity. As God had joined Himself to unfaithful Israel—exchanging covenant vows with them, caring for them, adorning them with blessings—so Hosea would join himself to an unfaithful wife.

The story doesn't end there, however. God next told Hosea to pursue his wayward wife, bring her home, and love her—just as God persistently continued to love His wayward people.

Yes, God judged Israel for their spiritual adultery, sending them into well-deserved exile. Yet even in the midst of pronouncing their doom, God, through Hosea, reaffirmed His love for His people and promised that they would one day be reconciled to Him forever.

One-sided love? Certainly. And thank God for it. For when we fail to live up to our vows, our faithful and forgiving Groom pursues us and keeps us with a love that cannot fail.

The Minor Prophets

When we come to Hosea, we enter a section of Scripture unfamiliar to many Christians: the Minor Prophets. To dispel some

HOSEA

	PERSONAL: The Agony of an Unfaithful Mate		NATIONAL: The Tragedy of an Unfaithful People		
	CHAPTERS 1–3		*CHAPTERS 4–14*		
	Marriage Children Separation Reunion		Series of sermons declaring the sin of the people and the character of God Model of the message as Hosea remains true to his wife in spite of her infidelity		
	Adulterous wife yet faithful husband		Adulterous nation yet faithful God		
	God: *"Go, take to yourself a wife of harlotry and have children of harlotry."* (1:2)	God: *"Go again, love a woman who is loved by her husband, yet an adulteress."* (3:1)	Nation is guilty	Nation needs judgment	Nation has hope
			God is holy	God is just	God is love
Theme	God's faithful love toward His unfaithful people				
Key Verses	2:19–20; 3:1; ch. 11				
Christ in Hosea	Christ's being "called out" from hiding in Egypt as a child is pictured in Hosea's record of Israel's exodus from Egypt (11:1; see also Matt. 2:15). In Hosea's redemption of Gomer from the slave market, Christ is pictured as the loving, faithful Redeemer of sinful humanity.				

of the mystery surrounding these final twelve books of the Old Testament, let's look briefly at their message and history.

Minor Prophets with a Major Message

In the Hebrew Bible, the Minor Prophets were combined into one book, called The Twelve, because of their brevity. However, as Bible scholar Irving L. Jensen explains, they

> are "minor" only in the sense of being much shorter than such prophecies as Isaiah and Jeremiah (called "major prophets"). Their message is surely not less important today, nor was it when first delivered in Old Testament times. They were minor prophets preaching a major message.[1]

Indeed, the Minor Prophets echo the Major Prophets' declarations and depictions of God's justice, holiness, judgment, mercy, comfort, grace, and salvation. They may be small in size, but they're big in truth.

When Did They Prophesy?

The Minor Prophets are not arranged chronologically, and no one is certain what determined their order in the canon. (With the help of the chart at the front of the guide, we can better grasp the eras in which they ministered.) The following lists show the differences between the scriptural order and the most likely chronological order.

Canonical Order	Chronological Order
Hosea	Obadiah
Joel	Joel
Amos	Jonah
Obadiah	Amos
Jonah	Hosea
Micah	Micah
Nahum	Nahum
Habakkuk	Zephaniah
Zephaniah	Habakkuk
Haggai	Haggai
Zechariah	Zechariah
Malachi	Malachi

---

1. Irving L. Jensen, *Jensen's Survey of the Old Testament* (Chicago, Ill.: Moody Press, 1978), p. 392.

After Malachi, the last of the Old Testament prophets, God didn't raise up another prophet until John the Baptizer, some four hundred years later.

Hosea: The First of Scripture's Minor Prophets

Author

Hosea, son of Beeri, was the only one of the writing prophets to come from the northern kingdom of Israel.[2] We don't know much about him, other than what he revealed in his book, because he is mentioned nowhere else in Scripture.

Sometimes known as the prophet of "Israel's zero hour," Hosea urged the northern kingdom to repent in its tragic final days before it fell to Assyria—much like Jeremiah's ministry to the crumbling kingdom of Judah more than a century later. He strove valiantly, and at great emotional cost, to live up to the calling of his name, which meant "salvation."

Historical Context

Authors Bruce Wilkinson and Kenneth Boa explain the circumstances surrounding Hosea's ministry.

> When Hosea began his ministry, Israel was enjoying a temporary period of political and economic prosperity under Jeroboam II. However, the nation began to crumble after Tiglath-pileser III (745–727 B.C.) strengthened Assyria. . . . Four [of Israel's last six kings] were murdered and a fifth was carried captive to Assyria. Confusion and decline characterized the last years of the northern kingdom, and her people refused to heed Hosea's warning of imminent judgment. The people were in a spiritual stupor, riddled with sin and idolatry.[3]

"'What we see in the prophecy of Hosea,'" they continue, quoting another commentator, "'are the last few swirls as the kingdom

---

2. Throughout Hosea, the northern tribe of Ephraim is synonymous with the whole northern kingdom of Israel.

3. Bruce Wilkinson and Kenneth Boa, *Talk Thru the Old Testament*, vol. 1 of *Talk Thru the Bible* (Nashville, Tenn.: Thomas Nelson Publishers, 1983), p. 235.

of Israel goes down the drain.' This book represents God's last gracious effort to plug the drain."[4]

Hosea was a contemporary of Jonah, whom God sent to the Assyrian capital of Nineveh; of Amos, who prophesied to the northern kingdom; and of Isaiah and Micah, who ministered to the southern kingdom. Hosea's ministry lasted around forty years, from about 755 to 715 B.C. His references to Judah (for example, the kings of Judah in 1:1) suggest that he may have fled to Jerusalem after the destruction of the northern kingdom and compiled his prophecies into one book there. It could be that he hoped the southern kingdom would learn from Israel's mistakes.

Structure and Theme

The entire book of Hosea centers on one theme: God's faithfulness to His unfaithful people. The theme is vividly played out in real-life drama in chapters 1–3, as Hosea, following God's command, takes a wife and then pursues her in love after she commits adultery.

The events in Hosea's life symbolize how Israel has committed spiritual adultery against the Lord with whom she had covenanted. In chapters 4–14, God delineates the nation's infidelity, calls her to repent, foretells judgment, and promises that He will forgive her and take her back to Himself.

Commentator Robert B. Chisholm Jr. has also noted "five judgment-salvation cycles" in Hosea—five movements that delineate God's case against His people but also offer the hope of restoration.[5]

Judgment	Salvation
1. 1:2–9	1:10–2:1
2. 2:2–13	2:14–3:5
3. 4:1–5:14	5:15–6:3
4. 6:4–11:7	11:8–11
5. 11:12–13:16	chap. 14

Hosea's Love for an Adulterous Wife (Chaps. 1–3)

Hosea probably had a stranger start to his ministry than any other prophet.

---

4. Wilkinson and Boa, *Talk Thru the Old Testament*, p. 236.

5. Robert B. Chisholm Jr., "Hosea," in *The Bible Knowledge Commentary*, Old Testament edition, ed. John F. Walvoord and Roy B. Zuck (Wheaton, Ill.: Scripture Press Publications, Victor Books, 1985), p. 1378.

The Unfaithfulness of Gomer and Israel (Chaps. 1–2)

> When the Lord first spoke through Hosea, the Lord said to Hosea, "Go, take to yourself a wife of harlotry, and have children of harlotry; for the land commits flagrant harlotry, forsaking the Lord." (Hos. 1:2)

As chapter 1 opens, Hosea, his wife Gomer, and even their children were to be a living lesson to unfaithful Israel about her deplorable spiritual condition.[6] Hosea was about to feel on a temporal scale what God was feeling on an eternal scale.

In addition to the object lesson of Hosea and Gomer's painful marriage, the children's names had lessons to teach. Jezreel, meaning "God scatters," Lo-ruhamah, meaning "not loved," and Lo-ammi, meaning "not my people" reveal the rift Israel's spiritual adultery had created between them and God as well as the nation's coming judgment.

God, however, didn't leave Hosea on such a despairing note. He reassured him that this alienation would not last forever, but would transition into future restoration. Israel would "be like the sand of the sea" (v. 10), a promise that echoes God's covenant with Abraham (see Gen. 13:16; 15:5; 32:12). A day would come when God would again call Israel "my people" ("Ammi") and "my loved one" ("Ruhamah") (Hos. 2:1).

With his first judgment-restoration cycle completed, Hosea launched into the next. From 2:2–13, he rebuked Israel for not acknowledging

> the Lord as the Source of her produce and wealth. Instead she used silver and gold to manufacture Baal idols (cf. 8:4; 13:2), for it was this Canaanite deity to whom she attributed her agricultural . . . and economic prosperity (2:5, 12–13).[7]

---

6. Did God tell Hosea to marry a prostitute, thus violating the moral standards of His own laws (see Lev. 19:29; Deut. 23:17–18; Prov. 2:16–19; 6:23–26; 23:26–28)? Bible scholars differ in their interpretation of this issue. Some see Hosea's marriage strictly as an allegory of Israel's unfaithfulness to the Lord. Others believe God literally commanded His prophet to marry a prostitute. Still others contend that God told Hosea to marry a woman who would become an adulteress and prostitute after he married her. This last view seems most accurate in light of the original Hebrew, which can be rendered, "Go, take to yourself a wife who will prove to be unfaithful." See Chisholm, "Hosea," p. 1379.

7. Chisholm, "Hosea," p. 1384.

Because Israel served her idols with God's gifts, the Lord would strip the land of its resources and leave it destitute—the covenant curse for not following the One true God (2:9, 12; see Deut. 28:23–24, 38–40).

But the promise of restoration, once again, is never far behind the pronouncement of judgment. Hosea reminded the Israelites that God would take them back like a forgiving husband . . . and love His bride forever (Hos. 2:14–23).

Restoration and Reconciliation (Chap. 3)

God's goal for His people was not destruction but restoration, as Hosea emphasized again.

> Then the Lord said to me, "Go again, love a woman who is loved by her husband, yet an adulteress, even as the Lord loves the sons of Israel." (3:1a)

This command, when we understand how far Gomer had fallen, would be easier said than done. Apparently, Gomer had become a slave, perhaps the property of someone who was hiring her out for prostitution. She might have even become a cult prostitute at a pagan temple and could only leave if compensation were paid to cover her services. So Hosea had to buy back his own wife.

By going after her, taking her off the street, and bringing her back into his home and heart, Hosea provided an unparalleled portrait of the indomitable nature of God's covenant love.

Once restored to Hosea, Gomer was to leave her promiscuity behind; she was to have no more lovers. Likewise, exiled Israel would no longer depend on foreign allies or worship false gods (v. 4). Ultimately, they were to

> seek the Lord their God and David their king; and they will come trembling to the Lord and to His goodness in the last days. (v. 5)

God's Love for an Adulterous People (Chaps. 4–14)

The remainder of the book expands on the infidelity theme introduced in the first section. Here God exposes the particular sins of Israel, showing how she had committed adultery with other gods and surrounding nations and abandoned the caring and just treatment of her own people. God would judge Israel's sins, but He would also pursue her in love, bring her home, and renew His relationship with her.

The Case against Israel (Chaps. 4–5)

Echoing his previous statements of judgment, Hosea laid out God's charges very specifically.

> Listen to the word of the Lord, O sons of Israel,
> For the Lord has a case against the inhabitants
>   of the land,
> Because there is no faithfulness or kindness
> Or knowledge of God in the land.
> There is swearing, deception, murder, stealing and
>   adultery.
> They employ violence, so that bloodshed follows
>   bloodshed. (4:1–2)

The people kicked aside God's Law, and even the priests and prophets pursued evil (vv. 4–10, 18–19). God's children had discarded His covenant for cheap and dangerous thrills. How could Israel not be judged? Judah, too, would face God's punishment (5:10). Restoration, though, not annihilation, was God's goal: "In their affliction they will earnestly seek Me" (v. 15).

Repentance Urged and Ignored (Chaps. 6–8)

As always, God left the door open for His wayward people to come back to Him. Hosea pleaded, "Come, let us return to the Lord" (6:1). But the Israelites' fickle passions kept them from any serious thoughts of repentance. Their loyalty drifted like a morning cloud and dried up like the dew (v. 4).

Though they assumed God didn't see their wickedness, their sins were "before [His] face" (7:2). "Ephraim mixes himself with the nations" (v. 8), trusting in them instead of God for strength and protection. Because of their persistent sin, Israel would fall to Assyria, who would swoop down upon them "like an eagle" (8:1). Israel had sown the wind and would reap the whirlwind (v. 7). The futility of their sin, in other words, would yield a crop of destruction.

The Certainty of God's Judgment (Chaps. 9–10)

Because Israel had become unclean, God would deport them to an unclean land, where they would eat unclean food and offer unclean sacrifices (9:1–9). Israel, once God's delight, had become

8

detestable to Him because they worshiped the god Baal-peor (v. 10). Worship to this pagan deity involved engaging in sexually immoral fertility rites. Ironically, God's punishment would bring the covenant curses of infertility, bereavement, and exile upon the nation (vv. 11–17; see also Deut. 28).

With judgment in sight, Hosea pleaded with Israel to seek the Lord:

> Sow with a view to righteousness,
> Reap in accordance with kindness;
> Break up your fallow ground,
> For it is time to seek the Lord
> Until He comes to rain righteousness on you.
> (10:12)

Unfortunately, the stubborn people did just the opposite: "You have plowed wickedness, you have reaped injustice, You have eaten the fruit of lies. Because you have trusted in *your* way" (v. 13, emphasis added).

The Rebellious Ultimately Restored (Chaps. 11–14)

The final four chapters remind us that God, though a righteous Judge, is also a faithful and forgiving Husband. Even though Israel had played the harlot, God never forgot that He had made a covenant with her . . . forever. God is faithful, even when His people are not.

His faithfulness to Israel, in fact, began before they were a nation—before they even left Egypt during the Exodus (11:1). In a switch of metaphors, Hosea said God adopted Israel as a son, and raised him as His own. But he rebelled and worshiped false gods. So he would be a slave once again—this time in Assyria (v. 5).

God promised, however, to bring His children back from Assyria to the Promised Land (11:8–11). His compassionate heart would not let Him abandon His people.

Chapter 12 begins the last pronouncements of judgment. Trusting in their wealth, the proud Israelites disregarded God. Lies and violence characterized the nation, and they fooled themselves into false security by making foreign alliances. To humble them, God reminded them of their lowly origins and confronted them with their guilt (12:1–14), their idolatry (13:1–3), and their forgetfulness of Him (vv. 4–6). But a day would soon come that would write His name on their hearts forever, etched there in the pain of the severe judgement He would inflict on them (vv. 7–16).

In chapter 14, though, Hosea rolls the stone of judgment away and basks in the new day of God's reconciling love. Upon Israel's return to Him, God would "heal their apostasy" and "love them freely" (v. 4). Israel would once again flourish, like a sturdy tree pruned by God's judgment and watered with His forgiveness (vv. 5b–7). And God's people would know once again that "it is I who answer and look after you" (v. 8).

As we take in the awesome message of Hosea, may we stay true to Him who loves us—who wooed us, won us, and will never leave us.

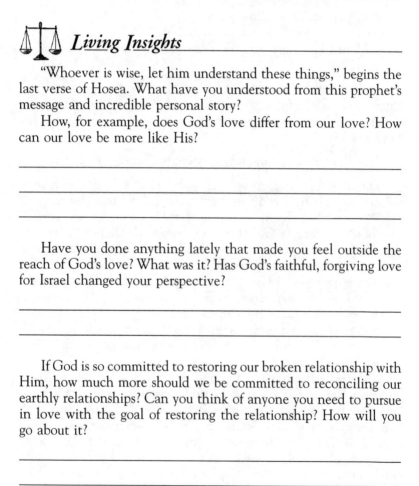 **Living Insights**

"Whoever is wise, let him understand these things," begins the last verse of Hosea. What have you understood from this prophet's message and incredible personal story?

How, for example, does God's love differ from our love? How can our love be more like His?

_____

_____

_____

Have you done anything lately that made you feel outside the reach of God's love? What was it? Has God's faithful, forgiving love for Israel changed your perspective?

_____

_____

If God is so committed to restoring our broken relationship with Him, how much more should we be committed to reconciling our earthly relationships? Can you think of anyone you need to pursue in love with the goal of restoring the relationship? How will you go about it?

_____

_____

_____

When was the last time you really forgave someone? When were you last forgiven? Is it time for either? Or both?

_____

_____

_____

We know what sin does to us. Has Hosea's story told you anything about what it does to God?

_____

_____

Have you wandered away from your first love? Been walking the streets (spiritually speaking)? If so, it's not too late to come home. The door is open. And so are His arms.

Chapter 2

JOEL: PREPARING FOR THE DAY OF THE LORD

A Survey of Joel

The black widow. The scorpion. The rattlesnake. The grasshopper.

Grasshopper? What's so scary about a grasshopper? Well, nothing, if you're just scooping one up in a jar. But to those who raise crops for a living, the grasshopper—or locust—is feared more than any other creature. Because when they come in swarms, they eat every bit of vegetation in their path—a ravenous, black cloud of destruction.

One wave of hungry locusts can rapidly reduce a flourishing green crop to a brittle skeleton of sticks. With no consideration for anyone or anything but their appetite, they strip the farmer of his livelihood . . . and move on to the next meal. The locusts' feast is the farmers' famine.

It shouldn't come as any surprise, then, that God chose the locust as an instrument of judgment for the sinful nation of Judah. Since Judah's society revolved around an agricultural economy, attacking their crops might get their attention and turn them back to God.

The prophet Joel urged his people to consider the locusts' ravenous fury and repent to avoid future judgments. For God devastates His people, not to drive them away, but to draw them near. He brings us to nothing so that we will run to Him who is everything. And through our repentance, He can turn famine into feast.

Author

About a dozen men in the Bible bear the name Joel, which means "Yahweh is God." All we know of Joel the prophet, son of Pethuel, is recorded in the book he wrote—and the prophet tells us very little about himself. His book reveals great concern for Judah and Jerusalem (see 2:32; 3:1, 6, 8, 16–21), so it is likely that he resided in and ministered to the southern kingdom.

Date

Joel mentions no datable historical events, so the time frame of his composition is uncertain. Among the clues scholars have

JOEL

	The Plague of Locusts	The Call to Repentance	The Future of Judah
	The past plague	"Return to Me"	Concerning the Spirit of God
	The future invasion	The character of God KEY: 2:13	Concerning the judgment of God
	Historic Day of the Lord	The universal appeal	Concerning the kingdom of God
	Imminent Day of the Lord		Ultimate Day of the Lord
		One of the greatest promises of hope in all the Old Testament	
	CHAPTERS 1:1–2:11	*CHAPTER 2:12–17*	*CHAPTER 2:18–27*	*CHAPTERS 2:28–3:21*
Emphasis	Desolation	Exhortation	Restoration
Emotion	Mourning now		Rejoicing later
Parallel Verse	"For His anger is but for a moment, His favor is for a lifetime; Weeping may last for the night, But a shout of joy comes in the morning." (Psalm 30:5)		
Theme	"Repent, for the Day of the Lord is near."		
Key Verses	2:12–14, 18, 25–27		
Christ in Joel	The coming of the Holy Spirit, who applies Christ's redemption, is predicted in 2:28. Jesus Christ is the One who judges nations, but also restores His people.		

13

sifted through to try to determine Joel's date are: the names of enemy nations included in (or excluded from) the book, the lack of kings' names, the reference to Judah as a scattered nation (3:2b), references to the temple (1:9, 13; 2:17), linguistic parallels to other prophetic books, and Joel's position in the canon.

Some scholars date the book as early as the ninth century B.C. In that case, Joel would have served in Judah about the same time Elisha was prophesying in Israel. Others place Joel in the late sixth century, just before Babylon's invasion of Judah, which would have made him a contemporary of Jeremiah. Still others argue for a postexilic date, positioning Joel with the other prophets—Haggai, Zechariah, and Malachi—who served the returned remnant after the Babylonian captivity.

Because each of these views has some merit, we simply cannot date the book with certainty.

Interpretational Challenges

Joel's lack of datable events makes interpreting the three-chapter book a challenging experience for any Bible student. Two main themes affect one's understanding of Joel: the meaning of the locusts and the "day of the Lord."

Locusts: Literal or Figurative?

What are we to make of the locust plague in Joel? Was it an actual insect invasion, or was it a figure for another event—perhaps a military attack? Scholars differ. "Historically," says the *New Geneva Study Bible,*

> the majority of interpreters have understood the lo-
> custs as symbols of future enemies. . . . But
> present-day interpreters see these creatures, at least
> in ch. 1, as actual locusts. Joel indeed moves quickly
> from an accurate description of a real devastation
> by locusts in ch. 1 to a description of the dreadful
> locust-like army of the Lord that blends the literal
> and figurative in ch. 2. It seems then that the de-
> struction by locusts that Joel had seen became the
> vehicle for his prophecy proclaiming the need to
> repent in view of the coming day of the Lord.[1]

1. *New Geneva Study Bible*, gen. ed. R. C. Sproul, Old Testament ed. Bruce Waltke (Nashville, Tenn.: Thomas Nelson Publishers, 1995), p. 1382.

In other words, Joel would have delivered his prophecy to Judah between two occasions of judgment: a past locust plague (chap. 1) and a locust-like military invasion yet to come (chap. 2).

The Day of the Lord

The main theme of Joel is "the day of the Lord" (1:15; 2:1, 11, 31; 3:14), a phrase that has broad usage and meaning in prophetic writing. Within the book of Joel itself, the "day of the Lord" has wide scope. In 1:15, 2:1, and 2:11, "it refers

> to a day of the Lord's wrath against Israel, though later in the book it refers to the Lord's wrath against the nations and blessing of the Lord's people (2:31; 3:14).[2]

"Generally speaking," writes commentator Robert B. Chisholm Jr.,

> "the day of the Lord" is an idiom used to emphasize the swift and decisive nature of the Lord's victory over His enemies on any given occasion. In the Old Testament "the day of the Lord" may refer to either a particular historical event or an eschatological [end times] battle which will culminate the present age.[3]

The locust invasion on Judah, then, was a day of the Lord. The impending invasion of Judah by a northern army would also qualify as a day of the Lord. The great Day of the Lord, however, will occur when Jesus Christ returns to bless His people and judge His enemies.

Survey of the Book of Joel

Joel begins with devastating judgment and ends with the promise of a glorious future for Israel.[4] A horde of locusts wreaks destruction in chapter 1, foreshadowing an invasion from a vicious army (2:1–11). In light of the impending military invasion, Joel delivers a heartfelt plea to repent (vv. 12–17). God promises full deliverance

---

2. *New Geneva Study Bible*, p. 1386, fn. on 1:15.

3. Robert B. Chisholm Jr., "Joel," in *The Bible Knowledge Commentary*, Old Testament edition, ed. John F. Walvoord and Roy B. Zuck (Wheaton, Ill.: Scripture Press Publications, Victor Books, 1985), p. 1412.

4. When we use the name Israel in the context of future restoration, we're not referring to the northern kingdom but to the eventual regathered and regenerate people of God.

and restoration (vv. 18–27), which will have its ultimate expression when Christ returns to bless His people and destroy His enemies (2:28–3:21).

The Day of the Locusts (Chap. 1)

Joel directs the people of Judah to ponder a recent locust invasion and pass its lessons on to future generations (1:1–3). The land is desolate, the devastation complete. Not a morsel of vegetation remains (v. 4).

The plague has affected every segment of society. All those touched by the devastation are instructed to mourn. The drunkards are to mourn, because there are no more grapes for making wine (vv. 5–7). The priests mourn, because there's no grain or wine left for temple offerings (vv. 8–9). The land itself mourns over its barrenness (v. 10). The farmer and vinedresser mourn, for there is no harvest (v. 11). The land is dried up; and with it, the people's joy (v. 12).

Joel instructs the whole nation to cry out to the Lord in their distress, to "consecrate a fast, Proclaim a solemn assembly" (v. 14). Fasting is often associated with repentance in Scripture, so this may be proof that the locust plague served as God's judgment on Judah.

An even greater day of judgment, however, is on the way:

> Alas for the day! For the day of the Lord is near,
> And it will come as destruction from the Almighty.
> (v. 15)

Joel, unlike Hosea and other prophets, doesn't list Judah's sins. We know from the rest of Scripture, though, that Judah's history is filled with idolatry, greed, social injustice, and overall disobedience to the Law.

Verses 16–20 close the chapter with a final reflection on the extent of the locusts' damage and serve as a transition into a description of another approaching day of the Lord.

The Imminent Day of the Lord (2:1–11)

"Blow a trumpet in Zion," warns the prophet (2:1). For the day of the Lord is coming. A day of "darkness and gloom" (v. 2) even worse than the locust invasion. This time, the army would be a powerful invading force from the north (v. 20).

This army's assault on Judah will resemble the locust invasion in number, destructive power, and immunity to defenses. As the dawn spreads itself over the earth, this army will cover Judah (v. 2). It will thunder across the land, strip its resources, and invade its homes (vv. 5–9).

Who is this army? It could have been the Assyrians, if Joel wrote in the ninth century. The Assyrian army sacked Samaria and tried to overthrow Jerusalem as well. God, however, rescued Jerusalem when King Hezekiah sought the Lord's help (see 2 Kings 18:13–19:37).

If Joel prophesied during Jeremiah's day, though, he would most likely have been referring to the ensuing Babylonian invasion in the late sixth century, which would fit the kind of fierce judgment depicted in Joel—although the Babylonian army was not routed in response to Judah's repentance (compare Joel 2:20).

If Joel were writing to postexilic Judah, he might have been describing a future Greek or Roman military conquest of the Middle East. Again, a lack of discernible dates makes it difficult to tell. Joel's main point is that judgment has come to Judah in the form of a locust invasion, is yet to come through a military invasion, and will ultimately come through the final cataclysmic intervention of the Lord.

The Call to Repent (2:12–17)

In light of past and coming judgments, Joel calls the people to repent and return to the Lord:

> "Yet even now," declares the Lord,
> "Return to Me with all your heart,
> And with fasting, weeping and mourning;
> And rend your heart and not your garments."
> Now return to the Lord your God. (vv. 12–13a)

Mere portrayals of remorse were not enough to stay God's judgment. Only hearts broken over sin could do that.

Joel echoes the other prophets in balancing God's judgment with His grace:

> For He is gracious and compassionate,
> Slow to anger, abounding in lovingkindness
> And relenting of evil. (v. 13b)

God's judgment is a waiting, wise judgment. It is never at the mercy of an irrational temper, impulsiveness, or misinformation. It always responds at exactly the right time and in exactly the right measure. And when His people repent, God's judgment steps aside to let mercy and grace flow.

Renewal and Restoration (2:18–27)

Not only does God promise to withhold judgment if Judah repents, He will restore all that they have lost to plague and war (2:19). God will destroy the northern army that threatens Judah (v. 20),[5] and will once again cause the land to flourish (vv. 21–25).

Once restored to God, the people's hearts will be as rich and full as the restored land. And God will once again be in their midst, the object of their praise and worship (vv. 26–27).

Did this time of restoration described in 2:18–27 occur in Joel's day? In part, perhaps. But Judah's no longer being a "reproach among the nations" (v. 19) presents some problems, because history shows that the nation of Israel has often been an object of scorn since Joel's day. Robert Chisholm is again helpful here:

> Perhaps the best solution to this difficulty is to understand that at least this aspect of the promise [Israel's scorn] is eschatological [pertains to the end times] in its ultimate fulfillment. . . . Prophecies pertaining to [Joel's] own generation are merged here with those that await future realization. This is common in Old Testament prophecies (e.g., Isa. 9:6–7; 61:1–2; Zech. 9:9–10).[6]

The Ultimate Day of the Lord (2:28–3:21)

Looking even further into the future, Joel foretells a time of ultimate and complete blessing for God's people and judgment for His enemies.

"This concluding section of the Book of Joel," writes Chisholm,

> develops more fully the [end times] element of the Lord's promise. . . . The deliverance experienced by Joel's generation foreshadowed that of the end times. The day of the Lord, so narrowly averted by

---

5. Many commentators see this "northern" army as the same one described in 2:1–11. Others believe this is a description of an attack on Israel in the last days before Christ returns. The army's being driven away and defeated would certainly apply to the Assyrians, who sacked Samaria but weren't able to take Jerusalem.

6. Chisholm, "Joel," pp. 1418–19.

Joel's repentant contemporaries, will come in full force against the enemies of God's people (perhaps foreshadowed by the northern army of 2:20). The promises of 2:19–27 will find their ultimate and absolute fulfillment as the Lord intervenes on Israel's behalf (2:28–32), decisively judges the nation's enemies (3:1–16a, 19), and securely establishes His people in their land (3:1, 16b–18, 20–21).[7]

The exact sequence and timing of these events is debated among theologians. A detailed exploration of Joel 2:28–3:21 and how it relates to Christ's return and the various views about the Rapture, the Tribulation, Israel and the church, and the millennial age lie beyond the scope of this chapter.[8]

We can, however, be certain of one thing. Jesus is coming back. And this time it won't be to die. It will be to bring in His kingdom, gather His people to Himself, and destroy all His enemies. It will be a dark day for those who oppose the Lord and have abused His people. The Lord will assemble them in the "valley of decision" (3:14). There they will arm for war but to no avail.

> Proclaim this among the nations:
> Prepare a war; rouse the mighty men!
> Let all the soldiers draw near, let them come up!
> Beat your plowshares into swords
> And your pruning hooks into spears;
> Let the weak say, "I am a mighty man."
> Hasten and come, all you surrounding nations,
> And gather yourselves there.
> Bring down, O Lord, Your mighty ones.
> Let the nations be aroused
> And come up to the valley of Jehoshaphat,
> For there I will sit to judge

---

7. Chisholm, "Joel," p. 1420.

8. For example, theologians differ about the meaning of God's promise to "pour out My Spirit" on all humanity (Joel 2:28). Peter's great sermon in Acts connects the Spirit's coming at Pentecost with Joel's words (see Acts 2:16–21); therefore, some say Joel's prophecy was fulfilled at Pentecost. Others see Pentecost as a partial fulfillment of Joel's words, believing that an even fuller empowering and filling of the Spirit will take place for believers during the Millennium, when Christ will reign on earth. They argue that Joel's words await complete fulfillment, since the cosmic upheaval described in Joel 2:30–32 didn't occur at Pentecost but will accompany Christ's return.

All the surrounding nations.
Put in the sickle, for the harvest is ripe.
Come, tread, for the wine press is full;
The vats overflow, for their wickedness is great.
(vv. 9–13)

To those who have put their trust in Christ, however, the Avenging Judge will be a refuge of comfort and blessing on that day.

Then you will know that I am the Lord your God,
Dwelling in Zion, My holy mountain.
So Jerusalem will be holy,
And strangers will pass through it no more.
And in that day
The mountains will drip with sweet wine,
And the hills will flow with milk,
And all the brooks of Judah will flow with water;
And a spring will go out from the house of the
    Lord
To water the valley of Shittim. (vv. 17–18)

The Day of the Lord will come. Are you ready?

🜲 *Living Insights*

Not all calamity is a result of God's judgment. Sometimes we're damaged by our own bad choices. We suffer, too, as a result of other people's choices. And other times, God brings hardship to mature us, show us His sufficiency, and demonstrate the faithfulness of His people. Whatever the cause, times of adversity provide an opportunity for us to examine our relationship with the Lord.

Take some time to consider whatever circumstances are troubling you right now. Write down one or two that are causing you the most anxiety.

_____

_____

_____

What insight can you glean from Joel about God's ability to bring good out of bad? Feast from famine? Wholeness from brokenness?

Abundance out of barrenness? A soft heart from a hard one?

_____

_____

_____

_____

_____

_____

_____

Now, how will you approach God with your troubles? What will you ask for? Why not do it now?

Chapter 3

AMOS: FROM FIG-PICKER TO PROPHET-PREACHER

A Survey of Amos

Most would say he wasn't cut out for the job. He was a sheep-herder, for goodness' sakes. A farmer. He was used to working with his hands, not delivering messages from heaven.

His senses were tuned to rural life—the smell of soil and sheep, the sting of sweat, and the skin-chiseling caress of wind and sun—not to the marble, gold, and satin of the royalty he would confront. By his own admission, Amos had no formal training for this daunting task.

> "I am not a prophet, nor am I the son of a prophet;
> for I am a herdsman and a grower of sycamore figs."
> (Amos 7:14)

But he possessed the one qualification necessary to preach God's message: he was called by God.

> "But the Lord took me from following the flock and
> the Lord said to me, 'Go prophesy to My people
> Israel.'" (v. 15)

So the man who led flocks went to the wandering sheep of Israel, confronting them with their empty religion, oppression of the poor, and total disregard for God's covenant commands. Time has not diminished the power of his words—nor their relevance.

The Man from Tekoa

Unlike Joel, the prophet Amos provided us with some specifics about his background and the era in which he ministered.

We know, first of all, that he was "among the sheepherders from Tekoa" (1:1), a rural town in Judea about eleven miles south of Jerusalem.[1] According to commentator Donald Sunukjian, the Hebrew word used for *sheepherders* in verse 1 is unique.

---

1. Alan R. Millard and John H. Stek, introduction to Amos, in *The NIV Study Bible*, ed. Kenneth L. Barker and others (Grand Rapids, Mich.: Zondervan Bible Publishers, 1985), p. 1345.

AMOS

Introduction	Oracles against the Nations	Sermons against Nation of Israel	Visions of Judgment	Promises of Hope
A sheepherder's vision	Damascus Gaza Tyre Edom Ammon Moab Judah Israel	"Hear this word . . . O sons of Israel (3:1) . . . you cows of Bashan (4:1) . . . O house of Israel" (5:1)	Locusts Fire Plumb line Ripe fruit The Lord by the altar	"In that day I will raise up the fallen booth of David. . . . I will also plant them on their land." (9:11, 15)
CHAPTER 1:1–2	*CHAPTERS 1:3–2:16*	*CHAPTERS 3–6*	*CHAPTERS 7:1–9:10*	*CHAPTER 9:11–15*

Theme	Israel's coming judgment for treating others with injustice
Key Verses	3:1–2; 4:12; 5:15, 24
Christ in Amos	Jesus Christ, who has all authority to judge, is also the one who restores His people.

[It] is not the usual Hebrew word *roeh*, but the rare word *noqed*, suggesting instead "sheep breeders." . . . Amos evidently managed or owned large herds of sheep and goats, and was in charge of other shepherds.[2]

Amos also described himself as a "herdsman" (7:14), which suggests that he was a rancher as well as a shepherd. As a "grower of sycamore figs" (v. 14), he tended

sycamore fruit, presumably as a sideline. . . . The sycamore did not grow in the heights of Tekoa, but only in the warmer lowlands, as the Jordan Valley and the fertile oases by the Dead Sea. Both of these places were near enough to Tekoa for Amos to super-vise the taking care of the trees (7:14)—a technical term that describes the process of slitting or scratch-ing the forming fruit so that some juice runs out, allowing the rest of the fig to ripen into a sweeter, more edible fruit. The three terms together indicate that Amos, as a breeder, rancher, and farmer, was a substantial and respected man in his community.[3]

Though Amos resided in Judah, his message was directed pri-marily to the northern kingdom of Israel. Crossing tribal boundaries to pronounce judgment, no doubt, made him even more unpopular than the average prophet. Yet Amos persisted to confront the sinful nation, lugging around God's weighty message and living up to the Hebrew meaning of his name—"Burden-Bearer."[4]

The Best of Times, The Worst of Times

During Amos' day, both Israel and Judah enjoyed a time of great power and prosperity. The threat from surrounding enemies was at an all-time low. King Uzziah of Judah, who reigned from about 790 to 739 B.C., "fortified Jerusalem and subdued the Philistines, the Ammonites, and the Edomites."[5]

2. Donald R. Sunukjian, "Amos," in *The Bible Knowledge Commentary*, Old Testament edition, ed. John F. Walvoord and Roy B. Zuck (Wheaton, Ill.: Scripture Press Publications, Victor Books, 1985), p. 1425.

3. Sunukjian, "Amos," p. 1425.

4. Bruce Wilkinson and Kenneth Boa, *Talk Thru the Old Testament*, vol. 1 of *Talk Thru the Bible* (Nashville, Tenn.: Thomas Nelson Publishers, 1983), p. 245.

5. Wilkinson and Boa, *Talk Thru the Old Testament*, p. 246.

To the north, Jeroboam II (793–753 B.C.) capitalized on the lack of aggression from Assyria, Aram, Syria, and Egypt to expand Israel's boundaries and increase trade. As a result,

> wealth began to accumulate in [Israel's] cities. Commerce thrived (8:5), an upper class emerged (4:1–3), and expensive homes were built (3:15; 5:11; 6:4, 11).[6]

This new prosperity, however, only led Israel further away from the Lord.

> The rich enjoyed an indolent, indulgent lifestyle (6:1–6), while the poor became targets for legal and economic exploitation (2:6–7; 5:7, 10–13; 6:12; 8:4–6). Slavery for debt was easily accepted (2:6; 8:6). Standards of morality had sunk to a low ebb (2:7). Meanwhile religion flourished. The people thronged to the shrines for the yearly festivals (4:4; 5:5; 8:3, 10), enthusiastically offering their sacrifices (4:5; 5:21–23). They steadfastly maintained that their God was with them, and considered themselves immune to disaster (5:14, 18–20; 6:1–3; 9:10).[7]

How wrong they were. Disaster—God's judgment—was on the way. Amos prophesied around 755 B.C. The Assyrians overtook Israel in 722, thirty years later.

As directed to his time as Amos' message was, his words could easily have been written to today's American church. We, too, have been blessed with prosperity, peace, and power. The question is, how are we using those blessings—to honor God, or to satisfy our own passions at others' expense?

Survey of Amos

Amos, like other prophetic books, communicates God's consuming holiness as well as His compassionate mercy. The bulk of the book, however, centers on Israel's sins, her well-deserved judgment, and her need to repent.

The first two chapters pronounce judgments, first against the Gentile nations, then on Judah and Israel. The middle section

---

6. Sunukjian, "Amos," p. 1425.

7. Sunukjian, "Amos," p. 1425.

(chaps. 3–6) highlights Israel's sins against the backdrop of God's efforts to get her attention and presents true repentance as the only way to escape His wrath. The prophet next reveals five visions of God's coming judgment (7:1–9:10). Finally, a picture of Israel's restoration (9:11–15) reminds the reader that not even God's severe judgment can make Him break His promise to retain a people for Himself.

Oracles against the Nations (Chaps. 1–2)

The first verse of chapter 1 introduces the prophet from Tekoa and orients us to his times. The earthquake he mentions, which occurred two years after his prophecy, rattled the people's resistance and reinforced the reality of God's coming judgment.

In verse 2, Amos portrays God as a roaring lion who has begun His attack on nations that have wronged Him (1:3–2:16). Commentator Thomas Edward McComiskey discloses a hidden significance in the order in which the nations appear.

> A striking pattern runs through these oracles. The prophet began with the distant city of Damascus and, like a hawk circling its prey, moved in ever-tightening circles, from one country to another, till at last he pounced on Israel. One can imagine Amos's hearers approving the denunciation of these heathen nations. They could even applaud God's denunciation of Judah because of the deep-seated hostility between the two kingdoms that went as far back as the dissolution of the united kingdom after Solomon. But Amos played no favorites; he swooped down on the unsuspecting Israelites as well in the severest language and condemned them for their crimes.[8]

Each pronouncement in these two chapters begins with the phrase, "Thus says the Lord," emphasizing the truth of the accusations against them and the certainty of God's judgment.

Another repeating phrase is "for three transgressions . . . and for four," which is a poetic device used in Scripture to convey fullness. God was judging these nations, not for one sin, but for to-the-core

---

8. Thomas Edward McComiskey, "Amos," in *The Expositor's Bible Commentary*, gen. ed. Frank E. Gaebelein (Grand Rapids, Mich.: Zondervan Publishing House, 1985), vol. 7, pp. 281–82.

sinfulness. The specific sins mentioned were the "last straw" that toppled God's patience.

Notice that in almost every pronouncement, the sin that drew God's judgment involved the mistreatment of other human beings—brutality, murder, oppression, exploitation, and the like. God's displeasure with those who mistreat others is a theme that runs throughout the book. In fact, it's a theme that runs throughout God's whole Book.

Sermons against Israel (Chaps. 3–6)

Having leapt from nation to nation with pronouncements of judgment, the Lord slows His pace to linger on the guilt of His chosen people. Commentator and pastor James Montgomery Boice explains why.

> Heathen nations have no special exemption from God's judgments, and Israel has no special position. The sermon that begins in chapter 3 picks up at that point, showing not only that Israel has no special position on the basis of which she can sin with impunity, but she actually has a higher obligation for holiness because of God's dealings with her and will therefore be judged more severely for her rebellion against God's law [see 3:1–2].[9]

The certainty of God's coming judgment is stressed through the list of questions He poses through His prophet (3:3–8). Each of the questions reflects a cause/effect relationship, hinting that Israel's sins have justly brought her own judgment.

Since Israel does not "know how to do what is right" (v. 10), an enemy, the Assyrians, will invade her land and ravage the people (vv. 11–12). Homes, buildings, idols—all the symbols of Israel's misdirected living—would come toppling down as well (vv. 13–15).

An incriminating portrait of the nation's sinfulness begins in chapter 4. Amos starts with the overindulged women of Israel, whom he sarcastically links to the "sleek cattle that grazed in the rich uplands of Bashan"[10] (v. 1). Their constant demand for comfort

---

9. James Montgomery Boice, *The Minor Prophets* (Grand Rapids, Mich.: Kregel Publications, 1986), p. 147.

10. McComiskey, "Amos," p. 302.

and luxury had kept food and clothing from the poor. Humiliation will replace their haughtiness, though, as these women will be led away by the enemy[11] through Samaria's breached wall (vv. 2–3).

Even the worship of the Israelites was self-centered, consisting of empty ritualism—a token nod to the God who had saved them (vv. 4–5). And although God had sent a variety of hardships upon Israel to get their attention and prompt their repentance (vv. 6–11), they would not return to Him. God's patience has run out: "'Prepare to meet your God, O Israel'" (v. 12).

Chapter 5 begins with a dirge or lament about Israel's forth-coming fate at the hands of the Assyrians (vv. 1–3). Still, God offers life to those who will seek Him in true repentance (vv. 4–6a; 14–15).

Israel's disregard for God's Law has surfaced in many ways. They pervert justice, exploit the poor to satisfy their lust for luxury, accept bribes, and oppress the righteous (vv. 7, 10–13). The Day of the Lord, which Israel mistakenly assumed would bring judgment for her enemies and joy for her, would be a time of swift and decisive judgment for her as well (vv. 18–20).

This spiritual hypocrisy of theirs was especially distasteful to God.

> "I hate, I reject your festivals,
> Nor do I delight in your solemn assemblies.
> Even though you offer up to Me burnt offerings
>   and your grain offerings,
> I will not accept them;
> And I will not even look at the peace offerings of
>   your fatlings.
> Take away from Me the noise of your songs;
> I will not even listen to the sound of your harps."
> (vv. 21–23)

Here's what He really wanted:

> "But let justice roll down like waters
> And righteousness like an ever-flowing stream."
> (v. 24)

Though they were rich, clean, and religious on the outside, their hearts were far from God. They had not "grieved over the ruin of

---

11. "According to Assyrian reliefs (pictures engraved on stone), prisoners of war were led away with a rope fastened to a hook that pierced the nose or lower lip." Millard and Stek, footnote on Amos 4:2, The NIV Study Bible, p. 1352.

Joseph" (6:6). Like the Pharisees of Jesus' day, they were whitewashed tombs, full of dead men's bones. Israel's arrogant, extravagant self-sufficiency would be her downfall (vv. 1–14).

Visions of Judgment (7:1–9:10)

God warns Amos of Israel's coming judgment through five visions. He does not bring about the first two, locusts and fire, thanks to Amos' intercessory pleading (7:1–6). The third vision, however, the plumb line, pictures God as measuring the sins of Israel against His perfect standards and finding the nation woefully crooked (vv. 7–9).

Possibly as a result of communicating this vision, Amos is confronted by Amaziah, a priest under Jeroboam II. "Get out, you seer!"—he shouts at Amos—"Go back to the land of Judah . . . and do your prophesying there. Don't prophesy anymore at Bethel, because this is *the king's sanctuary*" (vv. 12–13a NIV, emphasis added). What a pitiful testimony to how corrupt the worship had become.

Amos not only doesn't heed Amaziah's demand but prophesies in his presence about the doom the priest's family will face at the hands of the Assyrians (vv. 14–17).

In another vision, the Lord shows Amos a basket of ripe summer fruit, showing that the time is ripe for Israel's judgment (8:1–2). Part of that judgment will be the removal of God's life-giving Word, which they had disdained for so long (vv. 11–12).

In the final vision, the prophet sees the Lord standing beside the altar and pouring out destruction on the Israelites (9:1–10). No one escapes; God seeks out and destroys all those deserving of judgment. His standing by the altar may symbolize the sacrificial atonement provided in Christ—saying, perhaps, that those who reject the grace of God must face His judgment.

The Promise of Restoration (9:11–15)

Finally, a hopeful shaft of light pierces the gloom to reveal a future golden age when God will regather Israel in the land and reverse the covenant curses. "Behold, days are coming," the Lord promises, when

> "the plowman will overtake the reaper
> And the treader of grapes him who sows seed;
> When the mountains will drip sweet wine
> And all the hills will be dissolved.
> Also I will restore the captivity of My people Israel,

And they will rebuild the ruined cities and live
in them;
They will also plant vineyards and drink their
wine,
And make gardens and eat their fruit.
I will also plant them on their land,
And they will not again be rooted out from their
land
Which I have given them,"
Says the Lord your God. (vv. 13–15)

Yes, this rancher, sheepherder, and grower of sycamore figs was
used to working with his hands. But with his heart in God's hands,
what a greater work he performed.

 Living Insights
_____

The words of Amos can be uncomfortable to read, because they
probe beyond the thin veneer of religious activity and "playing
church." They remind us that a true love for God manifests itself
in a genuine love for people and a concern for their well-being.

Jesus said, "By this all men will know that you are My disciples,
if you have love for one another" (John 13:35).

The apostle John said, even more directly,

> If someone says, "I love God," and hates his brother,
> he is a liar; for the one who does not love his brother
> whom he has seen, cannot love God whom he has
> not seen. (1 John 4:20)

Another apostle, James, wrote,

> Pure and undefiled religion in the sight of our God
> and Father is this: to visit orphans and widows in
> their distress, and to keep oneself unstained by the
> world. (James 1:27; see also 1 John 3:17)

Enough Scripture; I'm getting convicted.

Amazing, isn't it, how we can pay lip service to God while
paying no mind to people created in His image. That's why God
judged the Israelites in Amos' day. They had all the trappings of
religion, but it was all a show. The godly characteristics that could

have helped their neighbors and revealed God to them—compassion, mercy, justice, righteousness—could never grow in a climate of hypocrisy.

We all need to take some time to think about how (or if) the love of God is seeping from the pores of our everyday lives. Do we view the homeless and destitute with contempt or compassion? Does our neighbor's divorce or job loss move us to prayer? Do we see the body of Christ as family members with real needs or as sinners to be tolerated?

Questions worth asking. And answering.

Chapter 4

OBADIAH: STRONG WARNING TO THE PROUD

A Survey of Obadiah

T he book of Obadiah, if assessed merely by its length, is the "most minor" of the minor prophets. It is the shortest book in the Old Testament.[1] In the symphony of Scripture, Obadiah seems to play an insignificant part. Like the tiny triangle, its few inspired notes can get lost among the singing strings and booming brass of more prominent books.

But don't let its size fool you. As the tiny triangle adds ringing, rhythmic tones to an orchestra's performance, so does Obadiah contribute beautifully to the Bible's message. Its twenty-one verses remind us in a powerful way that God stands by His redeemed; that He will indeed deliver the eternal blessings He has promised; and that the wicked who persecute God's people, though successful and secure for a time, will be brought to ruin by the Lord of heaven.

Obadiah is for anyone who needs a fresh reminder that, no matter who is against us, God is for us. And with us. Forever.

Author

Thirteen Old Testament figures bear the name Obadiah ("Worshipper of Yahweh" or "Servant of Yahweh"), but we cannot link any of the other twelve Obadiahs with any certainty to the writer of this book. The author provides no datable events or monarchs, so pinning down the exact period of his ministry is not possible.

The author's emphasis on Jerusalem suggests that he might have resided in the southern kingdom of Judah. Since his father is not mentioned, it's likely that Obadiah did not come from a kingly or priestly line but emerged from obscurity to proclaim God's message.

The Object of Obadiah's Oracle

Having waded through the scathing rebukes issued to Israel and Judah by some of the other prophets, you might be surprised to find

---

1. In case you were wondering, 3 John is the shortest book in the Bible.

OBADIAH

	Edom's Humiliation and Destruction	Edom's Cruelty and Crimes	Edom and the Day of the Lord
	VERSES 1–9	*VERSES 10–14*	*VERSES 15–21*
Portent	Prediction	Denunciation	Consummation
Event	What will happen	Why it will happen	How it will happen
Content	*"The arrogance of your heart has deceived you. . . . I will bring you down." (vv. 3–4)*	*"Because of violence to your brother Jacob . . ." (v. 10)*	*"As you have done, it will be done to you." (v. 15)*
Theme	The coming judgment of Edom		
Key Verse	"Because of violence to your brother Jacob, You will be covered with shame, And you will be cut off forever." (v.10)		
Christ in Obadiah	God's judgment of Edom and deliverance of Israel prefigure Christ's salvation and end-times judgment.		

that Obadiah contains no harsh words to either kingdom. Instead, Obadiah aimed his prophetic discourse at the nation of Edom, because they had delighted in Judah's downfall.

Edom and Israel: A History of Conflict

Just who were the Edomites, anyway? The nation crops up all over the Old Testament. In fact, commentator Walter L. Baker points out that

> judgment against Edom is mentioned in more Old Testament books than it is against any other foreign nation (cf. Isa. 11:14; 34:5–17; 63:1–6; Jer. 9:25–26; 25:17–26; 49:7–22; Lam. 4:21–22; Ezek. 25:12–14; 35; Joel 3:19; Amos 1:11–12; Obad.; Mal. 1:4).[2]

What did this nation, which bordered Judah to the east and south, do to arouse God's wrath? They were proud—arrogant and self-sufficient. But most of all, they looked down on and hated the chosen people of God—an animosity that went all the way back to the book of Genesis.

Jacob and Esau

Remember Isaac's twin sons, Jacob and Esau? Their sibling rivalry began in the womb of their mother, Rebekah.

> But the children struggled together within her; and she said, "If it is so, why then am I this way?" So she went to inquire of the Lord. The Lord said to her,
>
> > "Two nations are in your womb;
> > And two peoples will be separated from
> >   your body;
> > And one people shall be stronger than the
> >   other;
> > And the older shall serve the younger."
>
> When her days to be delivered were fulfilled, behold, there were twins in her womb. Now the first came forth red, all over like a hairy garment; and they

---

2. Walter L. Baker, "Obadiah," in *The Bible Knowledge Commentary*, Old Testament edition, ed. John F. Walvoord and Roy B. Zuck (Wheaton, Ill.: Scripture Press Publications, Victor Books, 1985), p. 1453.

named him Esau. Afterward his brother came forth with his hand holding on to Esau's heel, so his name was called Jacob; and Isaac was sixty years old when she gave birth to them. (Gen. 25:22–26)

As the boys grew into men, their differences became even more evident. Esau was a "skillful hunter, a man of the field, but Jacob was a peaceful man, living in tents" (v. 27). One day Esau, famished from working in the field, asked his brother for a swallow of red stew he had made. The request earned Esau the name Edom, which means "red." Jacob served up the stew, but only after Esau surrendered his birthright to him.[3]

Later, Jacob disguised himself as his older brother and received the family blessing from his blind and ailing father, Isaac. Enraged by Jacob's deception, Esau vowed to kill him. So Jacob fled for his life to Haran, the land of his mother's relatives.

Jacob remained in Haran, working for his uncle, Laban. Twenty years later (31:38)—with his wives, children, and possessions in tow—Jacob returned to Canaan. And Esau was waiting.

With an army of four hundred men, Esau rode to meet his returning brother on the road. Miraculously, it wasn't blood that flowed but tears as the two embraced (33:4). God had foretold Jacob's blessed status while the boys were still in the womb (25:23) and bestowed the Abrahamic covenant and protection on Jacob when he first fled to Haran (28:13–15). This wouldn't be the last time God would exercise His grace and protection over Abraham's chosen descendants.

From Brothers to Nations

Both Esau and Jacob initially settled in Canaan. Their respective families grew into nations—Esau's into Edom and Jacob's into Israel—and prospered so much that the land "could not sustain them" (36:7). So Esau moved to "the hill country of Seir" (v. 8), leaving Jacob all of Canaan. Though the twin brothers had

---

3. "The firstborn had the right to be the principal heir of the family's fortunes (27:33; Deut. 21:17; 1 Chron. 5:1, 2). In the covenant family, this fortune included the substance of the Abrahamic blessing of offspring and land (Gen. 12:2, 3, 7)." *New Geneva Study Bible*, gen. ed. R. C. Sproul, Old Testament ed. Bruce Waltke (Nashville, Tenn.: Thomas Nelson Publishers, 1995), p. 52, footnote on "birthright." By despising his birthright, Esau demonstrated his exclusion from God's covenant promises and affirmed God's sovereign selection of Jacob (see also Rom. 9:10–13; Heb. 12:14–17).

graciously reconciled, the two nations carried on the struggle that began in Rebekah's womb.

This animosity flared up generations later, after Israel was freed from 430 years of Egyptian slavery (Exod. 12:40–41). When Moses and the Israelites asked permission to pass through Edom on their journey to the Promised Land, the king of Edom said no and backed up his answer with a military barricade (Num. 20:14–21).

Pastor and author James Montgomery Boice tells of another clash between the two nations.

> David conquered the Edomites in a great battle recorded in 2 Samuel 8:13, 14, and from that time on through the reign of Solomon the Edomites were subject to the descendants of Jacob. One writer notes: "Until this time Edom must have been thought of as Israel's 'elder brother' in being stronger, older, and more developed. By this battle 'the elder' was 'supplanted' by 'the younger' in clear historical analogy to the Jacob-Esau parallel in Genesis. From this point on one can trace the bitter rivalry which is documented in the prophecy of Obadiah."[4]

The rivalry continued throughout the monarchy of the divided kingdom.

> In Jehoshaphat's reign Edom joined the Ammonites and the Moabites in an attack against Judah, but the attack ended with the Ammonites and Moabites defeating the Edomites (2 Chron. 20:1–2, 10–11, 22–26).
>
> In the reign of Jehoram, Jehoshaphat's son, Edom revolted against Judah and crowned their own king (2 Kings 8:20–22; 2 Chron. 21:8). Later Amaziah, king of Judah, crushed Edom, and changed the name of the city Sela to Joktheel (2 Kings 14:7; 2 Chron. 25:11–12). Later Edom attacked Judah during Ahaz's reign (2 Chron. 28:17). In 586 b.c. Edom encouraged Babylon to destroy Jerusalem (Ps. 137:7).[5]

4. James Montgomery Boice, The Minor Prophets, 2 vols. in 1 (Grand Rapids, Mich.: Kregel Publications, 1986), p. 190. Boice quotes John D. Watts, Obadiah: A Critical Exegetical Commentary (Grand Rapids, Mich.: William B. Eerdmans Publishing Co., 1969), p. 15.

5. Baker, "Obadiah," p. 1455.

The Edomites, driven from their land in the late sixth or early fifth century B.C. by the Nabateans, settled in Idumea (southern Judea). The Idumeans were eventually forced to become Jewish proselytes under John Hyrcanus, a Maccabean.[6] King Herod the Great, who tried to murder the baby Jesus, was an Idumean. In Jesus' protection from Herod's murderous rampage against Bethlehem's infants we have yet another illustration of grace toward Israel and judgment of Edom.

The Events in Obadiah

In Obadiah, then, what specific act of hostility against Judah did Edom delight in? Verses 10–14 provide the only historical reference, and the writer gives no dates. So scholars vary. Some say Obadiah is referring to Judah's being invaded and plundered by the Philistines and the Arabians during Jehoram's reign (848–41 B.C.; see 2 Chron. 21:16–17). Others believe Obadiah described the razing of Jerusalem under Nebuchadnezzar in 586 B.C.

Though the date is uncertain, Edom's impending doom was not. Let's look at Obadiah's words of judgment to this nation.

Survey of Obadiah

Verses 1–9 focus on the impending destruction of Edom. Verses 10–14 specify the charges against the nation. The Day of the Lord, when Israel will possess the land of her enemies, is foretold in verses 15–21.

The Judgment of Edom (Verses 1–9)

God revealed to Obadiah in a vision that He was declaring war on Edom, and He invited the other nations to join in the battle (v. 1). Though Edom was great in her own eyes, God would make her small (v. 2).[7] Her pride would be her downfall.

"The arrogance of your heart has deceived you,

---

6. Maccabee is another name for the Hasmonaeans, a prominent political Jewish family and sect from 166 B.C. to about 37 B.C. By Hyrcanus' death in 104 B.C., "the Jewish realm was at its greatest extent since Solomon's time." *New Bible Dictionary*, 2d ed. (1982; reprint, Downers Grove, Ill.: InterVarsity Press, 1991), p. 719.

7. This seems to have been accomplished, since the Edomites disappeared from history after A.D. 70. The ultimate judgment, though, for all nations that have oppressed God's people, will occur in the yet future "Day of the Lord" (see vv. 15–21).

You who live in the clefts of the rock,
In the loftiness of your dwelling place,
Who say in your heart,
'Who will bring me down to earth?'
Though you build high like the eagle,
Though you set your nest among the stars,
From there I will bring you down," declares the
    Lord. (vv. 3–4)

If ever a nation had a reason to feel self-sufficient, Edom did.
Two main factors, James Montgomery Boice explains, contributed
to her strength.

> First, [Edom] was situated along the great trade
> routes between Syria and Egypt and could profit from
> this trade. Trade brought business, and the inhabit-
> ants grew rich on tolls extracted from the many
> caravans. The second factor was Edom's natural
> strength and security. The central area is character-
> ized by red sandstone cliffs that rise to heights of
> more than 5,000 feet above sea level. These are
> easily fortified. As a result of having made their
> home within this natural fortress, the people of
> Edom were free to wage war and levy tribute on
> others while themselves being relatively free of out-
> side interference.[8]

The ancient fortress city of Sela (later known as Petra) was
virtually impenetrable. Experts say that, because of Petra's position
in the mountains, "it would be possible for a dozen men to hold it
against an army."[9] No wonder the Edomites could crow, "Who will
bring me down to earth" (v. 3)!

"I will," said God. His overthrow of Edom would be total; nothing would be left. Even thieves leave something behind when they
steal. And not even grape harvesters can get every single grape
(v. 5). But Esau "will be ransacked, And his hidden treasures
searched out!" (v. 6). God would even turn Edom's allies against
her (v. 7). Neither wisdom (v. 8) nor military might (v. 9) would
help Edom on that day.

8. Boice, *The Minor Prophets*, p. 189.

9. Boice, *The Minor Prophets*, p. 192.

The Charges against Edom (Verses 10–14)

Edom's violent cruelty toward Jacob's descendants would bring her from pride to shame (v. 10). God's action against Edom, though, wasn't arbitrary, as shown by the infallible evidence He produced.

Edom had stood by while enemies invaded Jerusalem and carried off her riches. The Edomites had even "cast lots," apparently to decide which portion of the ruined city to plunder. In this way, they were as guilty as the invaders (v. 11).

In addition, they gloated, rejoiced, and boasted over their "brother's" misfortune (v. 12). They swooped down from the rocks like vultures on the crippled city and carried off whatever remaining loot they could find (v. 13). And, to add insult to injury, the Edomites "actually caught Jews who were escaping from Jerusalem, rounded them up and then delivered them back into the hands of their enemies"[10] (v. 14).

Deplorable conduct for any neighboring nation! But the Edomites were brothers of the Judahites (v. 12). Both were descendants of Isaac. They were family. That made Edom's crimes all the more odious. As Obadiah announced next, however, a day would come when the nations would no longer trouble the Jews.

The Day of the Lord (Verses 15–21)

God's judgment of Edom typifies the Day of the Lord judgment facing all nations that oppose God and oppress His people.

> "For the day of the Lord draws near on all the
> nations.
> As you have done, it will be done to you.
> Your dealings will return on your own head.
> Because just as you drank on My holy mountain,
> All the nations will drink continually.
> They will drink and swallow
> And become as if they had never existed."
> (vv. 15–16)

Apparently, Edom had participated in a drunken celebration in Jerusalem when the city was overrun. They and the other nations would drink again—only next time the cup will be filled, not with wine, but with God's wrath.

---

10. Boice, *The Minor Prophets*, pp. 200–1.

With her enemies out of the way, the scattered Israelites will flock once again to the Promised Land, spread throughout it, and possess it as their own (vv. 17–20). "And the kingdom will be the Lord's" (v. 21).

God is for His people and with His people. He always has been. He always will be. What enemy, then, either national or spiritual, should we fear?

 Living Insights

Mountain fortresses. Military muscle. Strategic alliances. Human wisdom. They can make a nation powerful . . . and proud. That's why Edom came tumbling down from its lofty perch. When God decides to humble the proud, he targets the self-erected parapets that glorify human strength and stability.

It's not just the enemies of God, however, who need to guard against becoming prideful. As we've seen in the other prophetic books, God didn't tolerate Israel's or Judah's self-exalting, God-neglecting lifestyle either.

We need to remember that God wants us to be secure in *Him*, not in ourselves or our accomplishments. He alone is our Fortress, our Rock, our Shield, our Provider. How can we be proud when we realize that every blessing we have—whether material, spiritual, or relational—comes from His hand?

Got any human strongholds that are making you feel overly snug and smug? Maybe it's time to redirect your focus from the fortress to the Father. From your strength to His. From taking credit yourself to giving Him the credit. From accomplishment to adoration. From the riches you've amassed to the riches provided for you in Christ. And keep pride where it belongs—in the enemy's camp. Feel like writing? Here's some space to record your thoughts.

_____

_____

_____

_____

_____

Chapter 5

JONAH:
THE PRODIGAL PROPHET

A Survey of Jonah

What paragons of righteousness the prophets were. They spoke for God when no one else would. They stood alone against opposition. They wept aloud over sin. They prodded. They preached. They persevered. They ran away.

Ran away? Well, one prophet did. Jonah has the dubious honor of being the only prophet who ever rejected his commission from God and ran as fast as he could in the opposite direction. God caught up with him, though, and brought him to his knees. Then He used Jonah to bring about the greatest revival in history.

Jonah's story has much to teach us about God's sovereign control over all creation—including our individual lives—for His own glory. It also reveals His tender mercy, His compassion for the lost, and how He graciously employs us in His service . . . even when we fail Him.

And you thought Jonah was just a fish story!

Author

Jonah barely tells us anything about his life prior to his calling to Nineveh—only that he was the son of Amittai. We find a bit more history, however, in 2 Kings 14:25, which says that Israel's king Jeroboam II "restored the border of Israel . . . according to the word of the Lord, the God of Israel, which He spoke *through His servant Jonah the son of Amittai, the prophet, who was of Gath-hepher*" (emphasis added).

Jeroboam II reigned in the northern kingdom from 793–753 B.C. That means Jonah would have ministered in the northern kingdom[1] at least thirty years prior to Assyria's invasion of Israel in 722. Nineveh was the capital of Assyria. It's possible that Jonah had heard the message of Assyria's impending invasion from other

---

1. The town Gath-hepher mentioned in 1 Kings 14:25 was "three miles north of Nazareth in lower Galilee, making Jonah a prophet of the northern kingdom." Bruce Wilkinson and Kenneth Boa, *Talk Thru the Old Testament*, vol. 1 of *Talk Thru the Bible* (Nashville, Tenn.: Thomas Nelson Publishers, 1983), p. 256.

JONAH

	Running from God	Running to God	Running with God	Running against God
	First commission of Jonah	Prayer of Jonah	Second commission of Jonah	Prejudice of Jonah
	Results of disobedience	Communication with the Lord	Results of obedience	Lessons from the Lord
	CHAPTER 1	CHAPTER 2	CHAPTER 3	CHAPTER 4

Theme	God's infinite mercy for all people; our reluctance to share His mercy
Key Verses	2:9; 4:11
Christ in Jonah	Jonah's three days in the fish anticipates Christ's death and resurrection. The Ninevites' salvation represents the salvation available to all people in Christ.

prophets, such as Amos. If so, that may be one reason why he fled. After all, who wants to go share the gospel with one's future conquerors?

Historical Setting

Jeroboam II was one of the strongest military leaders in Israel's history. He expanded Israel's borders and ushered in a period of great peace and prosperity.

Peace and prosperity, however, led to pride. Because Israel was relieved of foreign pressures,

> she felt jealously complacent about her favored status with God. . . . She focused her religion on expectations of the "day of the Lord" . . . when God's darkness would engulf the other nations, leaving Israel to bask in his light.[2]

Perhaps that's why God sent Jonah to Nineveh—to squelch the national and spiritual smugness prevalent among the Israelites and remind them that they were to show His grace and mercy beyond their borders to all the nations of the world.

Interpretational Issues

The book of Jonah records some supernatural events that have raised questions about its historical credibility. Can a man really survive inside a fish for three days? Are we to believe that a whole city repented and turned to God so quickly and completely? And would God really cause a plant to grow overnight just to shade Jonah?

In addressing such questions, some interpreters classify the book of Jonah as an allegory, parable, or other type of nonhistorical, symbolic literature. Whether the events in Jonah actually happened, they say, is unimportant. What matters are the divine truths the symbols communicate.

Although the Bible does employ such literary forms (Jesus, for example, taught in parables), there's no good reason to approach Jonah's book as anything but actual history. Jesus certainly upheld the book's credibility when He referred to the prophet as a foreshadowing of His death and resurrection (see Matt. 12:39–41; Luke 11:29–32). Jewish tradition also regards Jonah's narrative as history.

2. Marvin R. Wilson and John H. Stek, introduction to Jonah, in *The NIV Study Bible*, ed. Kenneth L. Barker and others (Grand Rapids, Mich.: Zondervan Bible Publishers, 1985), p. 1363.

Besides, God created the universe—stars, planets, people, plants, animals—and reigns over it. He would certainly have no problem keeping a man alive inside a fish for three days. To dismiss such events as mere allegory is to deny the supernatural power of God.

> Skeptics can even look outside the Bible and find historical records of various large sea creatures swallowing a person whole. In one case, a man swallowed by a whale was still alive when he was removed.[3]

Style and Structure

Unlike most other prophetic portions of the Old Testament, Jonah is "a narrative account of a single prophetic mission."[4] It is a story of God's loving concern for all people. Nineveh, the great menace to Israel,

> is representative of the Gentiles. Correspondingly, stubbornly reluctant Jonah represents Israel's jealousy of her favored relationship with God and her unwillingness to share the Lord's compassion with the nations. The book depicts the larger scope of God's purpose for Israel: that she might rediscover the truth of his concern for the whole creation and that she might better understand her own role in carrying out that concern.[5]

The book can be divided according to Jonah's two commissions. He refused the first commission (chaps. 1–2). After being pursued and humbled by God, however, Jonah obeyed God's second command to preach to the Ninevites, though we find later that he still wasn't glad to do it (chaps. 3–4).

In chapter 1, Jonah runs *from* God to avoid preaching to the Ninevites. Chapter 2 finds him running *to* God for deliverance. In chapter 3, he's running *with* God, preaching the gospel in Nineveh. Even after his miraculous ministry, however, Jonah maintains a self-centered perspective on life. This causes him to run *against* God in chapter 4.

3. James Montgomery Boice, *The Minor Prophets*, 2 vols. in 1 (Grand Rapids, Mich.: Kregel Publications, 1986), vol. 1, p. 229.

4. Wilson and Stek, introduction to Jonah, p. 1364.

5. Wilson and Stek, introduction to Jonah, p. 1364.

Survey

Running from God (Chap. 1)

> The word of the Lord came to Jonah the son of
> Amittai saying, "Arise, go to Nineveh the great city
> and cry against it, for their wickedness has come up
> before Me." But Jonah rose up to flee to Tarshish
> from the presence of the Lord. So he went down to
> Joppa, found a ship which was going to Tarshish,
> paid the fare and went down into it to go with them
> to Tarshish from the presence of the Lord. (Jon. 1:1–3)

Nineveh was five hundred miles northeast of Gath-hepher,
Jonah's home town. Tarshish, a coastal city in what is now Spain,
was two thousand miles to the west, on the opposite end of the
Mediterranean Sea. What great measures Jonah took to avoid his
appointed task! Why? Why did he run?

We've already touched on the possibility that he didn't want
to share God's grace with an enemy prophesied to conquer his own
nation. Another reason could have been fear for his life. The Assyrians' reputation for cruel treatment of their enemies was wide-
spread. They were brutal and vicious, taking conquest to extremes
of torture and murder. Chapter 4, however, suggests that at least
part of Jonah's problem was his displeasure with the prospect of
God lavishing His grace on an undeserving, pagan nation. Jonah
didn't want the Ninevites saved; he wanted them judged. Jonah's
mercy, unlike God's, was limited by prejudice and pride.

Jonah never made it to Tarshish. God had other plans. Ironically, this uncompassionate prophet would be the very one to deliver
the message of God's compassion to the Ninevites. To bring this
about, the Lord sent a storm upon the sea . . . and into Jonah's life.

The storm God sent was fierce enough to terrify seasoned sailors
(v. 5). But Jonah, revealingly, was blissfully unaware of and uncon-
cerned about the others' peril. In his state of disobedience, he
managed to fall asleep.

Suspecting the storm to be an act of supernatural judgment, the
captain awakened Jonah and demanded that he "call on [his] god"
(v. 6). When the sailors cast lots and determined Jonah was to
blame for the storm, Jonah confessed to them his flight from God.

After he instructed them to throw him overboard to appease
God's wrath, the crew reluctantly tossed Jonah into the sea. The

storm subsided, the sea stopped raging, and the sailors believed in the Lord (v. 16). But where was Jonah?

Running to God (Chap. 2)

While God was at work on the surface, saving the sailors' souls, He was also at work in the depths, saving Jonah from drowning.

The Lord "appointed a great fish to swallow Jonah" (v. 17); and once inside the fish, Jonah understood that his plea for deliverance had been answered. Chapter 2 records the prayer of praise and repentance he uttered from inside his living prayer closet (vv. 2–9).

In Jonah's prayer, we find that he learned what we all do sooner or later—it is at our point of greatest weakness and helplessness that we realize our need for God most clearly. In the depths of the ocean, or the depths of despair, all we can do is cry out to Him. And He hears us.

God's intervention with Jonah brought more than mere physical deliverance; it brought spiritual renewal as well. Jonah recognized God's sovereign control over his life. The Lord not only cast him into the deep, He rescued him from it. Confronted with God's terrible discipline and sustained by His tender mercy, Jonah was ready to move toward God instead of away from Him.

> "Those who cling to worthless idols
>   forfeit the grace that could be theirs.
> But I, with a song of thanksgiving,
>   will sacrifice to You
> What I have vowed I will make good.
>   Salvation comes from the Lord." (vv. 8–9 NIV)

Having personally experienced the Lord's salvation, Jonah was now ready to preach it. So the fish, responding to the command of its Creator, "vomited Jonah up onto the dry land" (v. 10).

Running with God (Chap. 3)

What a sight this man on the beach must have been. He was probably pale and slimy from the fish's digestive fluids. His muscles most likely ached from three days in cramped quarters. And the sun, if it were out, would have been a sudden, searing reminder that people weren't meant to live in darkness.

The Ninevites, though, were still living in spiritual darkness, and they needed to be reached with the light of God's salvation.

So He gave His spokesman another chance, commissioning Jonah a second time:

> "Arise, go to Nineveh the great city and proclaim to it the proclamation which I am going to tell you." (3:2)

This time, Jonah responded with obedience.

> So Jonah arose and went to Nineveh according to the word of the Lord.[6] (3:3a)

Nineveh and its environs constituted a sprawling metropolis with perhaps as many as 600,000 people.[7] It would have taken "a three day's walk" (3:3b) to cover it all. Despite the size of his task, Jonah moved steadily through Nineveh with the message of God's impending judgment and His offer of repentance (v. 4).

Amazingly, the whole city—from the king down—repented of their wickedness, and God relented from His judgment (vv. 5–10). Through Jonah, God turned the hearts of the Ninevites to Himself, the single greatest revival history has ever known! But if you think this brought joy to Jonah, think again.

Running against God (Chap. 4)

> But it greatly displeased Jonah and he became angry. He prayed to the Lord and said, "Please Lord, was not this what I said while I was still in my own country? Therefore in order to forestall this I fled to Tarshish, for I knew that You are a gracious and compassionate God, slow to anger and abundant in lovingkindness, and one who relents concerning calamity. Therefore now, O Lord, please take my life from me, for death is better to me than life." The Lord said, "Do you have good reason to be angry?" (4:1–3)

All that saltwater hadn't washed away Jonah's spiritual haughtiness: "Why did you save these sinners, God? They should have

---

6. Nineveh lay inland from the Mediterranean Sea anywhere from 450 to 600 miles, depending on where along the coast the journey began. If the fish deposited Jonah near his hometown, the prophet would still have faced a journey of more than 500 miles to Nineveh.

7. Some commentators believe the figure of 120,000 in 4:11 refers to just one class of the population, such as young children.

been judged." He even had the audacity to treat God's goodness as if it were something bad.

The Lord could have given up on Jonah right here. But He wanted him to learn. "Do you have good reason to be angry?" asked the Lord. No answer.

So God exercised His power over creation once again. He made a plant sprout up to full size in a day to shade Jonah; then He sent a worm to destroy it. The hot wind and sun made Jonah miserable— so much so that he wanted to die. Again God asked, "Do you have good reason to be angry?"

"Yes," said Jonah. "Angry enough to die."

> Then the Lord said, "You had compassion on the plant for which you did not work and which you did not cause to grow, which came up overnight and perished overnight. Should I not have compassion on Nineveh, the great city in which there are more than 120,000 persons who do not know the difference between their right and left hand, as well as many animals?" (vv. 10–11)

Commentator John Hannah underscores the lesson in God's words.

> The vine was quite temporal . . . and was of relatively little value. Yet Jonah grieved over it. Whereas Jonah had no part in making the plant grow, God had created the Ninevites. Jonah's affections were distorted; he cared more for a vine than for human lives. He cared more for his personal comfort than for the spiritual destiny of thousands of people. What a picture of Israel in Jonah's day. . . .
>
> Whereas Jonah had thought God was absurd in sparing the Assyrians, God exposed Jonah as the one whose thinking was absurd.[8]

Interestingly, the book ends with God's question. We don't know how Jonah responded, or whether he ever shed his "spiritually privileged" attitude long enough to look at the lost the same way God did.

Have we?

---

8. John D. Hannah, "Jonah," in *The Bible Knowledge Commentary*, Old Testament edition, ed. John F. Walvoord and Roy B. Zuck (Wheaton, Ill.: Scripture Press Publications, Victor Books, 1985), p. 1472.

Salvation depends on God, not us. And it's a good thing. We're much less gracious than He is. Just look at Jonah, who took off for the open seas to keep from taking God's mercy to the Ninevites.

The Pharisees griped about Jesus' fraternizing with tax-gatherers and sinners. Yet the spiritually sick are the very ones who need God's healing touch the most.

Even the apostle Peter had to wrestle with an attitude of spiritual superiority. But God revealed to him that the Gospel was the great equalizer; the kingdom of God was open to Gentiles as well as Jews.

How about you? Is there anyone from whom you're withholding God's message of grace because you think that person doesn't deserve it? Are you keeping your distance from a neighbor, coworker, or family member because you would rather God give them "what they deserve" (judgment) than what they need the most (mercy)? Any names come to mind?

There are two ways to reach someone God wants you to reach: by sea (the long, hard way, through the waters of disobedience) or by land (still not easy, perhaps, but accompanied by the joys of following God's will). Take your pick.

By the way, aren't you glad God gives us what we need, not what we deserve?

Chapter 6

MICAH:
ADVOCATE FOR THE POOR

A Survey of Micah

What does God require of us?

Is it regular church attendance? Daily "quiet times"? Faithful Bible study? Determined Scripture memory? Cheerful tithing? Clean language?

These are all good things, activities and choices that can reveal a sensitive relationship with God. Some of them are even commanded in Scripture. But . . . does something seem to be missing? Something, perhaps, like life outside of ourselves? Or life outside of our church buildings?

True, we are not to be of the world—but we are still in it. We are set apart from the world, not in the sense of being withdrawn but of being *consecrated*. And God has consecrated us for a purpose: to be salt and light and guiding stars in our neighborhoods, businesses, communities, cultures, and societies.

In short, we are to live out our faith in *all* aspects of life. As Micah put it,

> He has showed you, O man, what is good.
> And what does the Lord require of you?
> To act justly and to love mercy
> and to walk humbly with your God.
> (Mic. 6:8 NIV)

Micah's book "emphasizes the integral relationship between true spirituality and social ethics."[1] Unfortunately, as we have seen so consistently in the historical books and the other prophets' writings, Israel and Judah missed this relationship. And in missing it, they missed out on the covenant blessings that could have been theirs.

They had traded beauty for ashes, but Micah was determined to turn them around.

---

1. Bruce Wilkinson and Kenneth Boa, *Talk Thru the Old Testament*, vol. 1 of *Talk Thru the Bible* (Nashville, Tenn.: Thomas Nelson Publishers, 1983), p. 263.

MICAH

	An Announcement of Judgment	A Contrast of Kingdoms	A Case against Sin and a Promise of Restoration
	"Hear, O peoples . . . Listen, O earth." (1:2)	*"Hear now, heads of Jacob And rulers." (3:1)*	*"Hear now what the Lord is saying." (6:1)*
	The capitals will be destroyed	Human corruption	God's indictment
	Reasons for judgment	Divine restoration	Authentic spirituality
			Judah's sins
			Messianic mercy
	CHAPTERS 1–2	*CHAPTERS 3–5*	*CHAPTERS 6–7*
Theme	Micah shows that a true relationship with God is inextricably linked to how we treat one another. He contrasts Judah's sinful kingdom with God's righteous and just messianic Kingdom.		
Key Verse	"He has told you, O man, what is good; And what does the Lord require of you But to do justice, to love kindness, And to walk humbly with your God?" (6:8)		
Christ in Micah	Jesus' birth in Bethlehem is predicted in 5:2; and His righteous reign over all the earth is described in 2:12–13; 4:1–8; 5:4–5.		

The Times

In the first verse of his prophetic message, Micah orients us to his times.

> The word of the Lord which came to Micah of Moresheth in the days of Jotham, Ahaz and Hezekiah, kings of Judah, which he saw concerning Samaria and Jerusalem. (1:1)

"The days of Jotham, Ahaz and Hezekiah" covered a span of years from about 750 to 686 B.C. During this time, the northern kingdom of Israel deteriorated under its last two kings. Pekah, who had assassinated the previous king, lost the bulk of Israel to Assyria's king Tiglath-pileser (2 Kings 15:25–29). "The ferocious onslaught against the northern tribes left only Mount Ephraim and the capital city of Samaria intact."[2] Hoshea assassinated Pekah and took the throne—only to be imprisoned by the next Assyrian king, Shalmaneser, and see Israel cease to exist as a nation in Assyrian exile of 722 B.C. (15:30; 17:1–6).

All this happened because Israel had adopted the ways of the surrounding pagan nations, served idols, and even made burnt offerings of their own children (vv. 7–17). They rejected the Lord's covenant and His righteous commandments and turned a deaf ear to His prophets. As the biblical writer sums up, "They followed worthless idols and themselves became worthless" (v. 15 NIV).

Judah, however, was doing somewhat better—at least for a while. The southern kingdom had peace and prosperity under righteous king Jotham, who reigned during the same time Pekah did in the north. Scripture tells us that "Jotham grew powerful because he walked steadfastly before the Lord his God" (2 Chron. 27:6 NIV). "The people," however, "continued acting corruptly" (v. 2b; compare Amos 1:1; 2:4–5).

Jotham's son Ahaz brought Judah to a new low. Following Israel's disastrous path, he turned to idols and sacrificed his own son in the fire. As a result, God withdrew His protection and allowed Aram and Israel to attack him and besiege Jerusalem. Israel's king Pekah killed 120,000 of Judah's soldiers in one day, with one of Ahaz's sons being among the casualties. Ahaz also lost six major cities and

---

2. "Campaigns of Tiglath-Pileser (745-732 B.C.)," in *The NIV Study Bible*, ed. Kenneth Barker and others (Grand Rapids, Mich.: Zondervan Bible Publishers, 1985), p. 550.

their surrounding villages to the Philistines. Rather than calling to the Lord for help, he sought out Tiglath-pileser, who made him a vassal of Assyria and "afflicted him instead of strengthening him" (2 Chron. 28:20b). Ahaz replaced the Lord's altar with a pagan one, dismantled the temple furnishings, and eventually closed the doors of the temple. In all this, the priests never opposed him but faithfully obeyed him instead (contrast with 26:16–18).

What a task Ahaz's son Hezekiah had ahead of him! Like her sister kingdom, Judah was far from the Lord, walking "in the customs which Israel had introduced" (2 Kings 17:19). So Hezekiah initiated radical change. He smashed the ubiquitous system of idolatry, re-opened the temple and began repairs, reinstituted the proper Levitical and priestly system, and celebrated a holy Passover to the Lord—with a remnant of true worshipers from the northern kingdom joining all of Judah.

However, even Hezekiah's righteous religious reforms could not entirely stem the tide of God's judgment and Assyria's rapacious greed. After Israel was carried off into exile, a later Assyrian king, Sennacherib, turned his hungry eye toward Judah. Attacking all her fortified cities and their surrounding villages, Sennacherib seized them and, he thought, control of Judah. The Lord, however, spared Jerusalem in answer to Hezekiah's heartfelt prayer, leaving the southern kingdom greatly compromised but still intact. Another threat loomed in the distance, though—Babylon would undo Judah due to Hezekiah's fateful pride and Judah's long history of national disobedience.

Such were the chaotic times in which Micah prophesied, along with his contemporaries Hosea, Amos, and Isaiah. The prosperity and resulting materialism in Jotham's day eventually gave way to oppression and desperate levels of corruption during Ahaz's and at least part of Hezekiah's reigns. The strong got stronger, and the weak grew weaker as the rules for living changed from God's standard to the demonic standards of idol worship. Before embarking into Micah's words, enter his world by reading the details of this history in 2 Kings 15–20; 2 Chronicles 27–32; and Isaiah 36–39.[3]

---

3. For an excellent description of the historical background of the eighth-century prophets (Jonah, Amos, Hosea, Isaiah, and Micah), see Thomas Edward McComiskey, "Amos," in *The Expositor's Bible Commentary*, gen. ed. Frank E. Gaebelein (Grand Rapids, Mich.: Zondervan Publishing House, 1985), pp. 269–70.

The Prophet

Little is known about the prophet Micah. His hometown, Moresheth, lay in Judah's fertile shephela foothills, near the fortified cities Lachish, Maresha, and Soco. It was about twenty-five miles southwest of Jerusalem and so close to the Philistine city Gath that it was often linked with this larger city and called Moresheth-gath.

Most commentators believe Micah was much like Amos, a small farmer or cattleman. Others see him as an important elder in Moresheth, viewing Moresheth itself as an important fortified city. And still others see him as a priest, like Jeremiah. We can surmise all we like, but the fact is, we really don't know. And that is as it should be, for, unlike Jonah, "what is important [in Micah] is the message rather than the messenger."[4]

The Message

Micah's message is essentially about "kingdom-of-God-living." Both Israel and Judah are condemned for violating the covenant standards of God's kingdom—for showing how God's people should *not* live. They were supposed to be a holy nation, a light to the Gentiles; instead, they chose to blend in with the surrounding darkness. Micah contrasts this upside-down picture with the right-side-up portrait of God's true kingdom, the ultimate Messianic kingdom, from which justice, truth, peace, safety, dignity, and mercy inherently flow.

The book of Micah, significantly, is bookended by God's character: It opens with His righteous judgment and closes with His faithful mercy. A subtle clue illuminates this for us—Micah's name (1:1). Meaning "Who is like Yahweh?" this theme starts and ends (7:18) the book.

We can outline the prophecy of Micah in a couple of ways, both of which are valid. First, we can structure it according to its subject matter: (1) the people's sins and coming judgment (chaps. 1–3), (2) ultimate messianic hope (chaps. 4–5), and (3) confronting and mourning for sins and ultimate restoration (chaps. 6–7). Another approach is to divide the book literarily, following Micah's three messages. These are signaled by the phrases, "Hear . . . Listen,"

---

4. Juan I. Alfaro, *Micah: Justice and Loyalty*, in the International Theological Commentary series (Grand Rapids, Mich.: William B. Eerdmans Publishing Co., 1989), p. 14.

(1:2), "Hear now . . ." (3:1), and "Hear now what the Lord is saying" (6:1). This last approach is the one we will take.

An Announcement of Judgment (Chaps. 1–2)

Following his brief introduction of himself in 1:1, Micah appropriately sets the stage with a gripping image of the Lord. Similar to Amos' beginning, Micah's introduction starts with a terrifying picture of God's power and judgment (vv. 2–5; compare Amos 1:2). Israel (represented by the capital, Samaria) receives God's condemnation first because of her history of unrelenting idolatry (Mic. 1:6–7). Mourning Israel's incurable wound of God's judgment, Micah is distressed to find that the wound has also come to Judah (vv. 8–9).

Judah was David's tribe and the kingdom in which his ruling line had been preserved. How fitting, then, that David's words of mourning, "Tell it not in Gath" (see 2 Sam. 1:20), and his place of hiding when he fled for his life, Adullam (see 1 Sam. 22:1), frame this next section detailing Judah's grief over impending exile (Mic. 1:10–16).

Micah makes a poignant play on words in verses 10–15, with each city relating ironically to its tragic destiny. In Gath, meaning "tell," they were to "tell it not." In Beth-le-aphrah, "house of dust," they were to roll in the dust of mourning. Those who lived in "pleasantness," Shaphir, were to leave their city most unpleasantly—in "shameful nakedness." Those who lived in "going out," Zanaan, would not get out ("escape"). The "house of removal," Beth-ezel, would have their support removed. Those who lived in "bitterness," Maroth, would face the bitter pain of God's judgment. The people of "team," Lachish, would harness their team to flee. On behalf of "betrothed," Moresheth-gath, they would give "wedding gifts as she passes from the rule of her own family to the authority of her cruel new husband, the invader."[5] The help of "deception," Achzib, would prove deceptive to Judah's king. And the people of "possessor," Mareshah, would be possessed by the enemy.

What had the people done to bring this calamity on themselves? The powerful had defrauded the poor of their homes, land, and ancestral inheritances, thus incurring God's wrath and depriving

---

5. James Montgomery Boice, *The Minor Prophets*, 2 vols. in 1 (Grand Rapids, Mich.: Kregel Publications, 1996), vol. 2, p. 18.

themselves of any further part in God's covenant community (2:1–5). The false prophets denied that God would ever be angry with His people, so they never tried to turn them from their sins. Consequently, they set the rich and powerful on a path of destruction, where they became ruthless enemies of the poor—and so of God—by their oppression and self-indulgence (vv. 6–11).

In contrast, God promises to gather a flourishing righteous remnant and guide them as a Shepherd-King to a place of peace and safety (vv. 12–13).

A Contrast of Kingdoms (Chaps. 3–5)

In the next section, Judah's corrupt shepherds and the society they have made (chap. 3) serve as the dark backdrop to the true Shepherd and the beauty of His ideal kingdom (chaps. 4–5). Micah has given us, in these latter chapters, some of the most precious pictures of Jesus the Messiah-King in all of Scripture.

Chapter 3 augments the picture of Judah's corruption by showing the brutal injustice of her leaders (vv. 1–3, 9–10), the treacherous greed of the false prophets (vv. 5, 11b), and the bribe-hunger of the judges and priests (v. 11a). In contrast, Micah used the power given him rightly—for the cause of justice, courage, and saving truth (v. 8). But because the people guiding the nation had chosen a path of wickedness, God would turn away from them and allow "Zion [to] be plowed as a field, Jerusalem [to] become a heap of ruins" (v. 12; also vv. 4, 6–7).

How different it will be when the Lord Himself reigns! In God's millennial kingdom, many nations will stream to Him to learn His law and His ways (4:1–3a). True justice will bring in lasting peace, where the people

> will hammer their swords into plowshares
> And their spears into pruning hooks;
> Nation will not lift up sword against nation,
> And never again will they train for war.
> (v. 3b; see also Isa. 2:1–5)

Justice, truth, peace, dignity, and mercy will be the hallmarks of God's kingdom—the opposite of what Judah had become. They would go to Babylon (vv. 9–10), but the Lord in His mercy would gather them again, ultimately giving His people victory in the millennial kingdom (vv. 10b–13).

In 5:1, Micah warns Judah to prepare for their future fight

against the Babylonians; but in verse 2, he looks to the future and foretells Christ—a ruler who would come from Bethlehem, who will one day gather scattered Israel (Israel and Judah will be a united nation once again) and deliver them in triumph from all their enemies (represented by "the Assyrian," verse 5). No longer will Israel rely on military power or the supernatural "power" of idols or the occult; the Lord will destroy these means and the cities that practice them, as well as disobedient nations (vv. 10–15).

A Case against Sin and a Promise of Restoration (Chaps. 6–7)

Before the silent, ancient witness of the mountains, the Lord next presents His case against His people and challenges them to find grounds of accusation against Him (6:1–3). To the charge of wearying them, the Lord defends Himself through evidence of His love: bringing them out of Egyptian slavery, setting godly leaders over them, turning curses into blessings, and leading them from Shittim across the Jordan River on dry ground into Gilgal and the Promised Land (vv. 4–5).

The people should have been humbled and changed by the evidence of God's greatness, but as we have seen, they were not. Commentator Juan I. Alfaro illuminates Micah's response in verses 6–8.

> The prophet, with heavy satire, puts on the lips of the sinful people an appropriate and superficial answer that seeks to avoid true conversion [v. 6]. . . . Does God prefer worship over justice? This question is often raised in the Prophets. . . . The divine answer will climax in Mic. 6:8, the most basic verse in the whole book of Micah. . . .
> . . . What does the Lord require from those who come to him? Micah points out that there is something worse than appearing before the Lord empty-handed (cf. Exod. 23:15; 34:20), namely appearing before him dirty-handed and empty-hearted.[6]

What the Lord wants is justice: "a commitment and a responsibility for the defense of the poor and the powerless so that they will not be victimized by the more powerful groups of society"; merciful kindness: "compassion and steadfast and loyal love, . . . a community-oriented activity, expressed concretely by protecting

6. Alfaro, *Micah: Justice and Loyalty*, pp. 66–67.

57

and helping those in need and through a spirit of solidarity"; and a humble walk with Him, which "is in direct opposition to the pride and presumption that drives persons to be self-centered and closed to everyone else"[7] (v. 8).

Unfortunately, external rituals devoid of the life-actions that make them meaningful were just what the people had become best at. Micah enumerates the injustices being perpetrated (vv. 9–12; compare with Lev. 19); then he proclaims God's judgment—a judgment designed to frustrate their desires and leave them as physically empty as they were spiritually (Mic. 6:13–15). As they had followed Israel's evil ways (symbolized by two of the northern kingdom's most wicked kings, Omri and Ahab), so they would follow her into judgment and destruction (v. 16).

"Woe is me!" Micah exclaims in light of this dismal situation (7:1). He mourns the sinful state of the land and the coming judgment (vv. 2–6), but he still finds hope—in the Lord, not in the people (v. 7). That God-rooted hope comprises the rest of Micah's message, as he predicts Israel's future restoration after judgment and repentance (vv. 8–9), her triumph and dignity, and her enemies' shame (vv. 10–13). He prays that God will shepherd His people as He did long ago, giving them a new exodus—a new beginning— that will lead them out of darkness into light and make their enemies fear the Lord (vv. 14–17).

In the end, it is God's pardon and forgiveness, His mercy and compassion, His casting away of sins and His faithfulness that Micah wishes to magnify. For like any true prophet, he did not want merely to announce judgment, to self-righteously condemn his people, but he wanted to turn them around and lead them to repentance and restoration. Even with all the judgments proclaimed, Micah's was a mission of mercy.

The Outcome

Was Micah successful in his prophetic endeavor? Unlike many prophets, whose messages seemed to bounce off hardened hearts, Micah's words bore godly fruit in two generations. The unheeded prophet Jeremiah must have been both grateful and wistful when he recorded this:

> Then the officials and all the people said to the

7. Alfaro, Micah: Justice and Loyalty, p. 69.

priests and to the prophets, "No death sentence for this man [Jeremiah]! For he has spoken to us in the name of the Lord our God." Then some of the elders of the land rose up and spoke to all the assembly of the people, saying, "Micah of Moresheth prophesied in the days of Hezekiah king of Judah; and he spoke to all the people of Judah, saying, 'Thus the Lord of hosts has said,

"Zion will be plowed as a field,
And Jerusalem will become ruins,
And the mountain of the house as the
    high places of a forest."'

Did Hezekiah king of Judah and all Judah put him to death? Did he not fear the Lord and entreat the favor of the Lord, and the Lord changed His mind about the misfortune which He had pronounced against them? But we are committing a great evil against ourselves." . . .

[So] the hand of Ahikam the son of Shaphan was with Jeremiah, so that he was not given into the hands of the people to put him to death. (Jer. 26:16–19, 24)

Not only did Micah's words spare his generation from Assyrian conquest, but decades later his testimony and the people's response to it saved the life of Jeremiah. Micah's mission was accomplished in those days.

Will it be accomplished in ours?

 Living Insights

What a rich study the little book of Micah is! It reveals to us so much of God's heart, His character, and His purpose for us. It still rings resoundingly with relevance for today.

For we, like Israel and Judah, are "a chosen race, a royal priesthood, a holy nation, a people for God's own possession, so that [we] may proclaim the excellencies of Him who has called [us] out of darkness into His marvelous light" (1 Pet. 2:9).

The riches given us in Christ have made us a privileged people—but there is a purpose in that privilege. We are to help others see the way out of darkness and into light (see John 14:6).

We can't do this, however, if our faith is too inward, if the light given us is clutched and hidden under the bushel of self-absorption or cliquishness (see Matt. 5:14–16). Our faith must reach out to the very real needs around us in this darkened world.

So ponder the message of Micah, and see how closely it relates to kingdom living under the New Covenant. Let the following passages guide you.

Matthew 7:21–23

Matthew 7:24–27

Matthew 25:31–45

James 1:27

---

1 John 2:9–11

---

1 John 3:17–18

---

1 John 4:20–21

Chapter 7

NAHUM:
THE CONSEQUENCES OF
NEGLIGENCE
A *Survey of Nahum*

What a difference a century can make!

Jonah, remember, had seen the entire city of Nineveh turn to God under his preaching around 760 B.C. But the generations who came after him neglected to build on that foundation of repentance. And the people of Nineveh became more evil and ruthless than ever before.

So a century after Jonah, God delivered another prophetic package to Nineveh through the prophet Nahum. This parcel, however, didn't contain the good news of mercy and grace. It was a heavy, black box. Foreboding. Unwelcome. Crammed full of divine judgment. And it was ticking.

The Ninevites were about to discover that, though God was a "gracious and compassionate God, slow to anger and abundant in lovingkindness, and one who relents concerning calamity" (Jon. 4:2), He also "reserves wrath for His enemies" (Nah. 1:2) and "will by no means leave the guilty unpunished" (v. 3).

Under Jonah, God's grace breached the walls of this mighty city. But Nahum tells of a day when God's judgment would bring them crashing down.

The Author

Nahum is another minor prophet about whom we know very little. He is not mentioned anywhere else in Scripture, and even the location of his hometown, Elkosh (1:1), remains a mystery to historians.

We do know that his name means "comfort." His message would have provided consolation, not for the doomed Ninevites, but for the Jews in Judah. As we saw in our previous chapter on Micah, the Assyrians had already destroyed Samaria and displaced the ten tribes. Twenty-one years later, they assaulted Judah, reinforcing her subservient position as a vassal state. Worse things had happened

NAHUM

	The Character and Power of God	The Judgment of God
	His majestic attributes and abilities in contrast to humanity's schemes	Predicted and described Justified and defended Inevitable and inescapable
	CHAPTER 1	*CHAPTERS 2–3*
Content	Theological	Prophetical
Emphasis	The majestic character of our sovereign God qualifies Him to be the Judge over all.	Nineveh's willful and heartless decline justifies the judgment of Almighty God.
Theme	The impending doom of Nineveh, capital of Assyria	
Key Verses	"And the Lord will by no means leave the guilty unpunished." (1:3b) "Woe to the bloody city." (3:1)	
Christ in Nahum	Christ will judge the nations, freeing His people once and for all from their enemies.	

in more recent days. In 2 Chronicles 33:11, we learn that the Assyrian army commanders captured Judah's king, Manasseh, put a hook through his nose, bound him with bronze shackles, and carried him off to the then-subordinate land of Babylon. How humiliating—and terrifying. To hear a message of this enemy's demise would have provided comfort indeed.

Since there is no evidence to suggest that Nahum traveled to Nineveh as Jonah did, his message was most likely proclaimed from his own soil, Judah.

Date and Setting

We can establish a general time frame for Nahum's ministry by gathering clues from within his book as well as from history. In chapter 3, he speaks of the destruction of No-amon, or Thebes, as having already happened (3:8–10). Assyria destroyed this city in 663 B.C.[1] In 612, Nahum's prophecy of Nineveh's fall came to pass as the Babylonians, Medes, and Scythians destroyed that great city. So Nahum must have delivered his message within that fifty-year span.

Because Nahum speaks of God's judgment as being imminent, some commentators suggest that he prophesied toward the end of this period. But it seems more likely that he ministered earlier, since he describes Nineveh at her height of power and prosperity, both of which began to wane toward the end of the seventh century B.C. Also, the city of No-amon was rebuilt in 654 B.C., so Nahum must have prophesied before that in order to use its destruction as an example of Assyrian cruelty. Nahum, then, probably ministered during the reign of Judah's wicked King Manasseh.

Nineveh had actually started to backslide long before Nahum came on the scene. In 722 B.C., just forty years after Jonah's visit, Sargon II of Assyria destroyed Samaria. One generation after Jonah—that's all it took for the Assyrians to return to wickedness.

Structure and Style

What's striking about Nahum's prophecy is the absence of an offer of repentance. Unlike Jonah, Nahum announces only judgment; he never once offers any chance to escape it. Using poetic

1. G. Herbert Livingston and Kenneth L. Barker, note on Nahum 3:8, in *The NIV Study Bible*, ed. Kenneth L. Barker and others (Grand Rapids, Mich.: Zondervan Bible Publishers, 1985), p. 1384.

repetition, Nahum threads the single theme of judgment throughout the book with skillful imagery and emotion.

His book can easily be divided into two main sections. Chapter 1 focuses on the character and power of God. Chapters 2 and 3 declare and defend God's judgment against Nineveh.

God the Judge (Chap. 1)

In his opening section, Nahum shows us the God who possesses power over all nature and creation and how He will use that power to destroy Nineveh.

> A jealous and avenging God is the Lord;
> The Lord is avenging and wrathful.
> The Lord takes vengeance on His adversaries,
> And He reserves wrath for His enemies.
> The Lord is slow to anger and great in power,
> And the Lord will by no means leave the guilty
>   unpunished.
> In whirlwind and storm is His way,
> And clouds are the dust beneath His feet.
> He rebukes the sea and makes it dry;
> He dries up all the rivers.
> Bashan and Carmel wither;
> The blossoms of Lebanon wither.
> Mountains quake because of Him
> And the hills dissolve;
> Indeed the earth is upheaved by His presence,
> The world and all the inhabitants in it.
> Who can stand before His indignation?
> Who can endure the burning of His anger?
> His wrath is poured out like fire
> And the rocks are broken up by Him.
> (1:2–6)

"A jealous and avenging God is the Lord." What did Nahum mean by that? First of all, we need to understand that God's jealousy and anger aren't like ours. He displays the sinless version of these qualities. He's not an out-of-control God who flies off the handle when He doesn't get His way.

Commentator Carl E. Armerding explains that these divine qualities, though they reveal a side of God we don't always like to talk about, are justified and just as necessary as His other attributes.

The adjective "jealous" . . . is used solely of God, primarily in his self-revelation at Sinai (Exod 20:5; 34:14). Against this covenantal background it denotes the Lord's deep, indeed, fiercely protective commitment to his people and his exclusive claim to obedience and reciprocal commitment (cf. Deut 4:24; 5:9). Where this relationship of mutual commitment is threatened, either by Israel's unfaithfulness or by foreign oppression, the inevitable expressions of such jealousy are "vengeance" and "wrath," directed to restoring that relationship (e.g., Num 25:11; Heb 10:27).[2]

While God "is good, A stronghold in the day of trouble, And He knows those who take refuge in Him" (1:7), He is "an overwhelming flood" to those who oppose Him and abuse His people (v. 8).

Nahum announces next that Assyria's plans to further oppress God's people would be thwarted.

Whatever you devise against the Lord,
He will make a complete end of it.
Distress will not rise up twice. (v. 9)

Assyria, though God's tool of judgment against Israel and Judah, would itself be judged for its brutal crimes. Soon it would be Nineveh's turn to be invaded, thrown into confusion, and brought to nothing (vv. 10–11). And the result of Nineveh's destruction would be Judah's deliverance and cause for great celebration (vv. 12–15).

Nineveh the Judged (Chaps. 2–3)

The next two chapters bring the judgment of Nineveh into even sharper view. Chapter 2 describes Nineveh's coming doom in vivid language. And, lest there be any doubt that God's judgment is just, chapter 3 paints a clear picture of Nineveh's sinfulness.

God mockingly calls on Nineveh to defend herself against "the one who scatters" who "has come up against you" (2:1). Scholars tell us this refers to the combined invasion forces of Nabopolassar of Babylon, Cyaxares the Mede, and the Scythians, who sacked Nineveh in 612 B.C. The stalwart defenses of Nineveh were no match for an army led by the Lord. Likewise, no nation can destroy a people God has chosen for Himself.

2. Carl E. Armerding, "Nahum," in *The Expositor's Bible Commentary,* gen. ed. Frank E. Gaebelein (Grand Rapids, Mich.: Zondervan Publishing House, 1985), vol. 7, p. 461.

For the Lord will restore the splendor of Jacob
Like the splendor of Israel,
Even though devastators have devastated them
And destroyed their vine branches. (v. 2)

The remainder of chapter 2 depicts the siege on Nineveh. Blood covers shield and soldier alike (v. 3). Invading chariots scramble through the streets like wildfire (v. 4). Assyrian soldiers stumble on the way to defend the city (v. 5). The attackers even use Nineveh's own water supply against it, opening up the gates that had held back this river and flooding the city (v. 6).

The city is plundered and her inhabitants exiled (vv. 7–10). Nineveh, once the jewel of Assyria, lays splintered, shattered, smoldering in the dust. Assyria, the lion who had preyed on other nations, is no match for the avenging Lord (vv. 11–13).

Why would God bring destruction on Nineveh? Author James Montgomery Boice writes,

> When Nahum calls Nineveh a "city of blood [3:1]," his words are a massive understatement. In all the ancient world no single city had matched the Assyrian capital for its calculated cruelty. . . .
>
> The utter fiendishness of impaling defeated soldiers on stakes, skinning commanders alive, cutting off limbs, noses and ears, putting out eyes, heaping up skulls in the city squares, and burning vast numbers alive was without parallel in the ancient world.[3]

Nineveh was also "full of lies and pillage" (3:1b). Its residents promised peace to cities they besieged but brought only destruction (see 2 Kings 18:13–37). And the wealth they possessed had been plundered from conquered nations.

Nahum 3:2–3 further describes the impending attack on Nineveh. As she has felled other cities, so she will fall—in a storm of charging chariots and flashing swords. As she "stacked corpses like cordwood by the gates of defeated cities,"[4] so her corpses will pile up on her streets. All "because of the many harlotries of the harlot,"

The charming one, the mistress of sorceries,

---

3. James Montgomery Boice, *The Minor Prophets*, 2 vols. in 1 (Grand Rapids, Mich.: Kregel Publications, 1986), vol. 2, pp. 67–68.

4. Livingston and Barker, note on Nahum 3:3, in *The NIV Study Bible*, p. 1384.

Who sells nations by her harlotries
And families by her sorceries. (v. 4)

Enticing other nations into alliance with her, Nineveh overthrew them later and stopped at nothing to satisfy her lust for power.
Nineveh also practiced witchcraft and sorcery, seeking power from
Satan himself. For these sins, Nineveh would suffer public shame—
look at how graphic Nahum's language is:

"Behold, I am against you," declares the Lord of
    hosts;
"And I will lift up your skirts over your face,
And show to the nations your nakedness
And to the kingdoms your disgrace.
I will throw filth on you
And make you vile,
And set you up as a spectacle.
And it will come about that all who see you
Will shrink from you and say,
'Nineveh is devastated!
Who will grieve for her?'
Where will I seek comforters for you?" (vv. 5–7)

Not a single person would grieve over Nineveh; not a single
person would offer comfort.

Nineveh's defenses would be useless against God's judgment,
just as the defenses of other nations had failed to protect them from
Assyria's aggression (vv. 8–10). Like drunkards (v. 11), the Ninevites would "be bereft of sense and direction under attack, frantically
seeking to hide."[5] All Nineveh's defenses will fall before the enemy,
as ripe figs fall from a tree when shaken (v. 12). The Ninevite
warriors will become as weak as women, allowing the city to be
entered and burned (v. 13).

In verses 15–17, Nahum uses the image of locusts three different
ways to show the totality of the destruction. First, even if the
Ninevites increase their numbers like locusts, no preparation for
the invasion will be able to stop the slaughter (vv. 14–15). Second,
the merchants within her walls will turn on the city, stripping it

---

5. Elliot B. Johnson, "Nahum," in *The Bible Knowledge Commentary*, Old Testament edition,
ed. John F. Walvoord and Roy B. Zuck (Wheaton, Ill.: Scripture Press Publications, Victor
Books, 1985), p. 1503.

like locusts strip fields (v. 16). And her leaders, like locusts that devoured the land and suddenly disappeared, will flee in fear, vanishing into oblivion (v. 17).

With the city destroyed and the leaders dead, the Ninevites will scatter like sheep, never to be regathered (v. 18). Nineveh the great will be reduced to ashes and never rise again[6]—a lamentable event for the Ninevites but joyful news for the nations she has ravaged.

> There is no relief for your breakdown,
> Your wound is incurable.
> All who hear about you
> Will clap their hands over you,
> For on whom has not your evil passed
> continually? (v. 19)

Concluding Thought

The wrath of God is a terrible thing. But for those who have put their trust in Christ, it's a reason for joy. It reminds us that God will punish the wicked and preserve His people. It also reminds us that we will not suffer the wrath of God. Jesus already did that for us on the cross.

Nineveh never rose again. But Jesus did. And because we are in Him, we are safe from the vengeful wrath of God—and secure in His loving grace and mercy.

 Living Insights

High profile court cases are a frustrating reminder that our society is not the best at dispensing justice. Our judicial system often seems more concerned about the criminal than the victim. But Nahum promises that

> the Lord takes vengeance on His adversaries,
> And He reserves wrath for His enemies. . . .

---

6. "Interestingly, for centuries no one knew where Nineveh itself lay buried; in 1845 it was finally uncovered by archaeologists." Livingston and Barker, note on Nahum 3:17, in *The NIV Study Bible*, p. 1385.

> And the Lord will by no means leave the guilty
> unpunished. (1:2–3)

Since God is the perfect Judge, He dispenses justice perfectly—just the right measure, at just the right time, to just the right people. There's no chance of God condemning an innocent person or inflicting a punishment that's too severe (or too lenient).

Are you involved in a situation right now in which you want to see justice done? (I'm talking about legitimate justice. Asking God to strike your husband with lightning because he forgot your anniversary doesn't count.)

Has someone in your family suffered at the hands of a criminal? Are you locked in a legal battle with someone who has taken advantage of you? Do you know of any pastors or other religious leaders who are taking advantage of their congregation?

You may feel as though your hands are tied, but God's aren't. What encouragement can you gain from Nahum about God's handling people whom you can't?

_____

_____

_____

Yes, God's a much better Judge than we are. Maybe that's why the apostle Paul said,

> Never pay back evil for evil to anyone. Respect what is right in the sight of all men. If possible, so far as it depends on you, be at peace with all men. Never take your own revenge, beloved, but leave room for the wrath of God, for it is written, "Vengeance is Mine, I will repay," says the Lord. (Rom. 12:17–19)

Remember, though, God may choose to delay judgment. He may even dispense mercy instead of judgment. It's His choice. But we can trust Him to do the right thing.

Chapter 8

HABAKKUK:
WRESTLING, WAITING,
PRAYING, PRAISING
A *Survey of Habakkuk*

"Behold the proud,
His soul is not upright in him;
But the just shall live by his faith."
(Hab. 2:4 NKJV, emphasis added)

If you were to ask the average churchgoer which biblical writers were most important to Christianity, it's doubtful that Habakkuk's name would ever come up. Yet this obscure prophet's words were used to form the foundation of our faith.

The apostle Paul drew upon Habakkuk 2:4 to argue that sinners are saved not by the Law but by faith in Christ alone (Rom. 1:16–17; see also Gal. 3:10–11).

Almost fifteen hundred years later, an Augustinian monk named Martin Luther agonized over how he, a sinful man, could be reconciled to a holy God who hates and judges sin. Desperately trying to gain God's favor, Luther performed all the church-prescribed rituals but found no relief—until, as he wrote later,

> God had mercy on me, and I began to understand that the righteousness of God is that gift of God by which a righteous man lives, namely, faith, and that this sentence—The righteousness of God is revealed in the Gospel [Rom. 1:17a]—is passive, indicating that the merciful God justifies us by faith, as it is written: "The righteous shall live by faith." Now I felt as though I had been reborn altogether and had entered Paradise. In the same moment the face of the whole of Scripture became apparent to me.[1]

Luther "had recovered the biblical doctrine of justification by

---

1. John Woodbridge, "Martin Luther: A Courageous Man of Faith," in *Tabletalk*, October 1992, p. 7.

HABAKKUK

	Habakkuk's Dialogue with God			Habakkuk's Praise to God
	The Burden	**The Watch**	**The Vision**	
	Wrestling with:	Waiting for an answer	Record the vision!	Lord, I've heard
	God's silence		Wait for it!	. . . I stand in awe
	Judah's sinfulness		Woe to the Babylonians!	. . . I wait
	God's character			. . . I praise
	Questions: How long? Who? Why? Who?			. . . I rejoice
	CHAPTER 1	CHAPTER 2:1	CHAPTER 2:2–20	CHAPTER 3
Confession	"Lord . . . You confuse me."		"Lord . . . I wait for You."	"Lord . . . I praise You."
Perspective	Horizontal	Vertical		
Direction	Looking around and worrying	Looking up and listening		Looking ahead and believing
Theme	Habakkuk's wrestling with God over His unfathomable ways and the prophet's resulting faith			
Key Verses	2:4; 3:17–19			
Christ in Habakkuk	Those who have been made righteous in Christ must "live by [their] faith" (2:4). When Christ comes again, "the earth will be filled with the knowledge of the glory of the Lord, as the waters cover the sea" (2:14).			

faith alone through grace,"[2] and with his spiritual rebirth, the Protestant Reformation was born in the year 1517.

Though Habakkuk's context was different from Paul's and Luther's, his words still clearly reveal that life flows from a steadfast faith in God rather than pride in our own strength (compare Eph. 2:8–9). And, as we shall see, Habakkuk's personal journey of faith—which culminates in praise-filled surrender to God—has much to teach us about putting our complete trust in God, though His ways often baffle us.

The Prophet

Who was Habakkuk? He identifies himself as "the prophet" in 1:1 and 3:1, which suggests

> that Habakkuk was a professional prophet. The clos-
> ing statement at the end of the psalm ("To the Chief
> Musician. With my stringed instruments.") suggests
> that Habakkuk may have been a priest connected
> with the temple worship in Jerusalem.[3]

His style indicates a well-educated and deeply sensitive man of God who was as poetic as he was prophetic.

The meaning of his name is uncertain, but the possibilities are intriguing. Some scholars connect the prophet's name with that of an Assyrian plant, the *hambakuku*, which could "suggest the pene-tration of Assyrian culture into Judean society."[4] Other linguists, however, trace the name back to the Hebrew word *habaq*, which means "embrace." His name, then, could mean "One Who Embraces (or Clings)." How appropriate, since, at the end of his book, Habakkuk "chooses to cling firmly to God regardless of what happens to his nation"[5] (3:17–19).

2. Woodbridge, "Martin Luther," p. 7.

3. Bruce Wilkinson and Kenneth Boa, *Talk Thru the Old Testament,* vol. 1 of *Talk Thru the Bible* (Nashville, Tenn.: Thomas Nelson Publishers, 1983), p. 273.

4. *New Geneva Study Bible,* gen. ed. R. C. Sproul, Old Testament ed. Bruce Waltke (Nashville, Tenn.: Thomas Nelson Publishers, 1995), p. 1442.

5. Wilkinson and Boa, *Talk Thru the Old Testament,* p. 273.

The Period

Despite Israel's fall to Assyria, God's repeated prophetic warnings to surviving Judah had gone unheeded. Soon the southern kingdom, too, would be judged.

Habakkuk's book lacks specific dates, but a pretty good case can be made that his dialogue with God occurred between 612 and 605 B.C. Habakkuk described the Babylonians (Chaldeans) as a world power, a position they achieved after they overthrew Nineveh in 612. Also, Nebuchadnezzar of Babylon attacked Jerusalem three times—in 605, taking hostages to ensure loyalty from the newly conquered Judah; in 597, to crush a rebellion led by Judah's King Jehoiachin; and in 586, burning Jerusalem to the ground and carrying the inhabitants into exile. Since Habakkuk presents Babylon's aggression against Judah as future, it seems unlikely that any of these attacks had yet occurred.

A few more clues can help us narrow the date even further. Habakkuk's description of Judah's sinfulness doesn't fit the period of spiritual reform under King Josiah (640–609 B.C.). It more accurately fits either the short reign of Jehoahaz (three months in 609 B.C.) or the wicked reign of Jehoiakim (609–598 B.C.).

Habakkuk's dialogue with God, then, probably took place between 609 B.C. (the end of Josiah's reign) and 605 B.C. (Nebuchadnezzar's first invasion of Judah). This would make Habakkuk a contemporary of Jeremiah.

Structure of Habakkuk

The book of Habakkuk begins with a sob and ends with a song. Its three chapters trace a personal struggle within Habakkuk rather than a public address to the people. Chapters 1–2 focus on Habakkuk's *dialogue with God*. Chapter 3 records the *praise to God*, he offered after working through what God had revealed to him about Babylon.

Dialogue with God (Chaps. 1–2)

First Question and Answer (1:1–11)

His soul burdened by Judah's flagrant sinfulness,[6] Habakkuk had been calling on God to take action against this people who now sneered at His covenant standards. Yet God had been silent—and,

---

6. The Hebrew word *oracle* (v. 1) can also be translated *burden*.

from Habakkuk's perspective, idle. Perplexed, he asked God,

> How long, O Lord, will I call for help,
> And You will not hear?
> I cry out to You, "Violence!"
> Yet You do not save.
> Why do You make me see iniquity,
> And cause me to look on wickedness?
> Yes, destruction and violence are before me;
> Strife exists and contention arises.
> Therefore the law is ignored
> And justice is never upheld.
> For the wicked surround the righteous;
> Therefore justice comes out perverted.
> (Hab. 1:2–4)

How, Habakkuk wondered, could God let His own people go on like this?

But God had not been idle. Justice was on the way—in a most surprising form: "Behold, I am raising up the Chaldeans, That fierce and impetuous people Who march throughout the earth To seize dwelling places which are not theirs" (vv. 5–6).

The Chaldeans' (Babylonians') character was "rooted in a self-sufficiency that acknowledged no superior authority and no dependency, which was tantamount to self-deification."[7] And this godless people would be God's scourge across the back of His own people. What divine irony! The sinners of Judah "were but soiled saints next to the barbaric Babylonians."[8]

> "They are dreaded and feared;
> Their justice and authority originate with
>   themselves." (v. 7)

Fierce, swift predators (v. 8), in their savage sweep across the landscape they preyed on other nations and "collect[ed] captives like sand" (v. 9). They scoffed at kings (v. 10), often putting captured royalty on humiliating public display—a brutality later epitomized

---

7. Carl E. Armerding, "Habakkuk," in *The Expositor's Bible Commentary*, gen. ed. Frank E. Gaebelein (Grand Rapids, Mich.: Zondervan Publishing House, 1985), vol. 7, p. 503.

8. J. Ronald Blue, "Habakkuk," in *The Bible Knowledge Commentary*, Old Testament edition, ed. John F. Walvoord and Roy B. Zuck (Wheaton, Ill.: Scripture Press Publications, Victor Books 1985), p. 1509.

at Jerusalem's destruction in 586 B.C. Nebuchadnezzar captured Zedekiah, Judah's last king, put his sons to death in front of him, then put out his eyes before taking him to Babylon in shackles (see 2 Kings 25:5–7).

No fortress could withstand the Babylonian army. They were skilled at building earthen siege ramps (Hab. 1:10). They would sweep through Jerusalem "like the wind" (v. 11). Yet, though appointed by God, they would still be held accountable for their ruthlessness.

Second Question and Answer (1:12–2:20)

Habakkuk's question, "How long, O Lord?" had been answered. Justice was on the way. But God's answer had him more perplexed than ever.

> Are You not from everlasting,
> O Lord, my God, my Holy One?
> We will not die.
> You, O Lord, have appointed them to judge;
> And You, O Rock, have established them to
>   correct.
> Your eyes are too pure to approve evil,
> And You can not look on wickedness with favor.
> Why do You look with favor
> On those who deal treacherously?
> Why are You silent when the wicked swallow up
> Those more righteous than they? (vv. 12–13)

Even though Habakkuk was familiar with God's covenant promises to preserve a people for Himself, and even though he knew all Judah would not be snuffed out ("We will not die," v. 12), the prophet was shocked by God's plan. How could God, whose eyes were "too pure to approve evil" (v. 13), choose such a wicked, merciless, and idolatrous nation to punish His own people (vv. 14–17)? Like Job of old, Habakkuk was stumped by God's apparent perversion of justice.

So he waited, as a sentinel standing watch, for the Lord to answer and untangle this knotty dilemma (2:1).

In response, God told Habakkuk to write down what He revealed to him, so that "the one who reads it may run" and herald the future judgment of Babylon that would "certainly come" and "not delay" (vv. 2–3).

The Babylonians would pay for their brutality—that was God's answer. Babylon, the "proud one," would be judged because he did not live as the righteous, "by faith" (v. 4).

The proud put their faith in themselves and are judged. The righteous put their faith in God and are blessed. That's true for nations and individuals. In salvation, we come to God by faith, relinquishing all our human attempts to gain His favor and putting our trust in His Son instead. We grow in Christ and walk with Him the same way—by faith. That is the path to blessing (compare Heb. 10:35–39).

The Babylonians, though, followed the faithless path of pride and self-gain. Like death and the grave, they could never get their fill of swallowing up weaker nations (Hab. 2:5).

Verses 6–20 further outline Babylon's coming judgment and the reasons for it. The nations, knowing Babylon's fate, will "take up a taunt-song" (v. 6) against him, sounding out his fate in a series of "woes" (vv. 6, 9, 12, 15, 19).

Babylon would suffer for making itself rich on other nations' wealth. Those whom they had looted would themselves plunder Babylon (vv. 6–8). Babylon, who had built a towering world empire by trampling on others, would be brought down (vv. 9–11). They had covered the known world with blood to build their empire (vv. 12–13). God's kingdom, in contrast, would fill the earth

> With the knowledge of the glory of the Lord,
> As the waters cover the sea. (v. 14)

As the Babylonians had taken advantage of and disgraced other nations for their own pleasure (v. 15), they, too, would be publicly shamed in drinking the cup of God's judgment (v. 16). Lebanon, exemplary of the nations Babylon had stripped of life and resources, would "overwhelm" her enemy (v. 17). Babylon would also be judged by the Lord for its idolatry. As "the stone and wood idols . . . are silent before the people," so "the people of the world are to be silent before the true God, who is about to judge"[9] (vv. 18–20).

Praise to God (Chap. 3)

The wicked and greedy Babylonians would be judged, but not

9. Roland K. Harrison and William C. Williams, note on Habakkuk 2:20, in *The NIV Study Bible*, ed. Kenneth L. Barker and others (Grand Rapids, Mich.: Zondervan Bible Publishers, 1985), p. 1390.

before they delivered judgment on Judah. Habakkuk's head must have been swimming from this revelation. But his heart could still trust in God.

In prayer, the prophet voiced his faith in God's justice as well as in His mercy (v. 2). Habakkuk then extolled God, who makes His magnificence known throughout the universe (vv. 3–7), controls all nature (vv. 8–11), and crushes wickedness while saving His people (vv. 12–15). Though terrified at the news of Babylon's invasion and the devastation it would bring (v. 16), Habakkuk knew he could trust the God of creation and salvation to do the right thing.

> Though the fig tree should not blossom
> And there be no fruit on the vines,
> Though the yield of the olive should fail
> And the fields produce no food,
> Though the flock should be cut off from the fold
> And there be no cattle in the stalls,
> Yet I will exult in the Lord,
> I will rejoice in the God of my salvation.
> The Lord God is my strength,
> And He has made my feet like hinds' feet,
> And makes me walk on my high places.
> (vv. 17–19)

Because Habakkuk knew the power and character of the living God, he could look to heaven when his world was falling apart. He could rest in Him . . . and so can we.

 *Living Insights*

Did you notice that throughout his conversation with God, Habakkuk continually reminded himself of God's attributes? God is eternal (1:12a). He is holy (v. 12b). He keeps His covenant promises ("We will not die," v. 12c). He is a Rock (v. 12d). He is pure, without sin (v. 13). He dispenses both wrath and mercy (3:2). He is all-powerful and sovereign over creation (vv. 3–12). He saves His people and destroys His enemies (vv. 13–14). He is the source of strength for His people (v. 19).

Though Habakkuk's book isn't a manual for how to pray, it certainly has a lot to teach us about prayer. It tells us, for one thing, that a major element of prayer must be a healthy perspective of who God is and how He has worked in history. Such a perspective reminds us that not only is God capable of handling our requests, but that He has been doing even mightier things for centuries.

A healthy picture of God also takes the self-centeredness out of prayer and puts our focus where it should be—on God. The better we know Him, the more we'll want what He wants, and the more concerned we'll be with His having His way in our lives. This doesn't mean we deny the reality of our struggles; Habakkuk certainly didn't hold back his feelings. But when God is our focus, our struggles become, not isolated islands of pain, but paths toward Him.

Read through Habakkuk's short book one more time, thoughtfully, making a list of God's attributes and abilities. The next time you need to bring a struggle before Him in prayer, start by reflecting on that list. Then pray with confidence that your prayers are heard by "Him who is able to do far more abundantly beyond all that we ask or think" (Eph. 3:20).

Chapter 9

ZEPHANIAH: BRIGHT LIGHT IN A DARK DAY

A *Survey of Zephaniah*

It was the disaster that no one thought would happen—or could happen.

The largest and most luxurious ship in the world, the RMS *Titanic* was the iron wonder of the Industrial Age, the pinnacle of human ingenuity. So confident in her prowess were some of her passengers that they claimed, "Even God couldn't sink this ship!"[1]

No one could foresee the catastrophe awaiting them in the icy waters of the Atlantic.

> The *Titanic* was four days at sea. It was April 14, a Sunday. She was speeding along, entirely too fast for a ship of her tonnage, as she approached the North Atlantic ice fields, but the ship's owners wanted to set an Atlantic crossing speed record. No safety drills had taken place.
>
> The wireless operators, busy arranging ticker-tape parades and parties that would celebrate the *Titanic*'s arrival in New York, ignored or made light of repeated warnings of icebergs in the ship's path. Even Captain Edward Smith, with more than 40 years of experience, seemed complacent. After all, he too thought the ship was unsinkable.[2]

Shortly before midnight, the crew spied an iceberg dead ahead. The liner veered left, avoiding a head-on collision but scraping the ship's hull along the iceberg's jagged undersea mass. The impact tore a three-hundred-foot gash along the ship's starboard side.

> Water quickly flooded the bow of the *Titanic*. Very few passengers, most of whom had retired for the night, had any clue what was happening. When they

---

1. Bob Garner, "Titanic," *Focus on the Family* magazine, April 1997, p. 1.

2. Garner, "Titanic," p. 1.

ZEPHANIAH

Judgment and Doom

"'I will completely remove all things From the face of the earth,' declares the Lord." (1:2)

Joy and Deliverance

	INTRODUCTION (1:1)	DIVINE JUDGMENT ON JUDAH *CHAPTER 1:2–18*	INVITATION *CHAPTER 2:1–3*	SURE DOOM OF NATIONS *CHAPTER 2:4–15*	SURE DOOM OF JERUSALEM *CHAPTERS 2:16–3:8*	KINGDOM PROMISES TO REMNANT *CHAPTER 3:9–20*
Scope		Judah		Nations		Remnant
Subject		Sin	Hope	Desolation		Restoration
Key Words		*"The day of the Lord"*	*"Seek"*	*"Woe"*		*"The Lord is with you"*
Theme		Judgment and doom are certain unless there is repentance before God. Only then can there be hope and restoration.				
Key Verses		"Near is the great day of the Lord, Near and coming very quickly; Listen, the day of the Lord! In it the warrior cries out bitterly." (1:14) "Seek the Lord, All you humble of the earth Who have carried out His ordinances; Seek righteousness, seek humility. Perhaps you will be hidden In the day of the Lord's anger." (2:3)				
Christ in Zephaniah		Jesus Christ hides us from God's wrath, and is the One who will someday rule the earth as King of Israel (Zeph. 3:15–17; see Col. 3:3–4).				

received word to begin boarding lifeboats, many joked about the bulky orange life jackets and giggled among themselves.

They were absolutely sure the *Titanic*'s watertight compartments would keep her from sinking until rescue boats arrived. It wasn't until the lifeboats had been lowered, the rocket flares had been launched, and the huge ship began listing and tilting forward that the passengers realized they were in serious trouble.[3]

The elegant vessel was equipped with only twenty lifeboats, far too few for the more than 2,200 passengers and crew. After the women and children were helped aboard, those left behind stood courageously on deck singing hymns as the ship went down. Finally, at 2:20 A.M., on April 15, 1912, the unsinkable *Titanic* heaved a final gasp and plunged bow-first into the freezing black waters of the North Atlantic sea. More than 1,500 lives were lost.

In many ways, the tragedy of the *Titanic* parallels the story of our world. We'd like to think that human ingenuity has made us safe from disaster, that we're too great to fall. But are we really? Under the surface, sin has ripped a gash in humanity's soul, and, whether or not we choose to believe it, we're sinking.

Zephaniah radioed an urgent message to the nation of Judah and is sending one to our modern world as well: *You're heading straight toward disaster.* But we need not despair—there's hope! Unlike the lifeboats on the *Titanic*, God's mercy and grace have room for everyone. All we need to do is climb aboard.

Zephaniah's Background and Times

Let's prepare to receive Zephaniah's message by taking a look at the man who sent it.

The Prophet

Zephaniah was the only prophet with a royal lineage. The first verse of the book reveals that he was a descendent of Hezekiah, the former king of Judah. Because of this, he most likely had access to the palace and may have been a personal adviser to the king.

---

3. Garner, "Titanic," p. 2.

The Prophet's Times

Zephaniah ministered during the reign of Josiah, who was the grandson of Judah's most wicked king, Manasseh. Manasseh's fifty-five-year reign had brought the level of national depravity to sickening new lows. He'd set up pagan altars and idols in the temple, sacrificed his own children in the fire, and fully embraced the occult (see 2 Chron. 33:2–7). He also "shed very much innocent blood until he had filled Jerusalem from one end to another" (2 Kings 21:16). In short, he "seduced [the people] to do evil more than the nations whom the Lord destroyed before the sons of Israel" (v. 9).

Though Manasseh humbled himself before the Lord after being taken captive by the Assyrians, his reforms had little transforming effect on his debased people (2 Chron. 33:10–17). Even his son Amon, his successor, followed his father's reprobate example instead of his repentant one and was assassinated by his own officials after ruling for only two years (vv. 21–25).

Clearly, Judah was on a disaster course, heading straight for God's judgment—unless someone could change the direction of the nation. That task fell to Amon's eight-year-old son, Josiah. When Josiah turned sixteen, "he began to seek the God of his father David" (34:3a). And when he turned twenty, "he began to purge Judah and Jerusalem of the high places, the Asherim, the carved images and the molten images" (v. 3b). Ultimately, with Assyria preoccupied with Babylon, Josiah expanded his influence to the north. The zealous young king swept through Palestine like a whirlwind, demolishing every altar and idol he could find.[4]

When the land was cleansed, he set about renovating the temple. Hilkiah the priest discovered a copy of the Law there, lost for decades, and presented it to Josiah. He wept as he read it and vowed to put it into practice. The priestly ranks and temple service were soon back in order, and God told Josiah He would stay His hand of judgment because of Josiah's humility before Him—but only for Josiah's lifetime (2 Kings 22:18–20; 2 Chron. 34:26–28).

As if to prove God's words, soon after Josiah's death in 609 B.C. the nation reverted to its previous sinful course. Four years later, in 605, Nebuchadnezzar made the first of his three invasions into Palestine. Josiah's revival had been only a brief detour in Judah's

---

4. Unknown to Josiah, God had long ago ordained his zealous actions (see 1 Kings 13:1–3; 2 Kings 23:15–16).

destiny with disaster, just as God had said (2 Kings 22:15–17; 23:25–27; 2 Chron. 34:23–25).

The Book's Date

Most scholars place Zephaniah's ministry either before or after the discovery of the Law in 622 B.C. If his prophecies came before, they would have coincided with Josiah's reform efforts and even contributed to them. If they came after, but prior to Nineveh's fall (compare Zeph. 2:13–15), they reveal the shallowness of Judah's revival and how quickly the people were sliding back into sin.

Zephaniah's Style and Purpose

To most people, Zephaniah comes across as a raging, fiery prophet. Most of his book booms and flashes like a terrifying thunderstorm. In fact, he preached about the Day of the Lord more than any other prophet—including Joel—referring to it more than twenty times in three chapters. However, as Matthew Henry perceptively observed, Zephaniah's purpose was not "to drive the people to despair, but to drive them to God and to their duty—not to frighten them out of their wits, but to frighten them out of their sins."[5]

Zephaniah's ultimate goal was to move the people beyond guilt to repentance. Listen to his desperate plea in 2:3—the centerpiece of the book:

> Seek the Lord,
> All you humble of the earth
> Who have carried out His ordinances;
> Seek righteousness, seek humility.
> Perhaps you will be hidden
> In the day of the Lord's anger.

Interestingly, Zephaniah's name means "Yahweh hides"—which was his message in a nutshell. The day of the Lord was coming; there was no stopping it now. But if the people would repent, God would give them a place to hide. He would preserve them *through* the hour of testing and usher them into His glorious kingdom.[6]

---

5. Matthew Henry, *Commentary on the Whole Bible*, ed. Leslie F. Church, one-volume ed. (Grand Rapids, Mich.: Zondervan Publishing House, 1961), p. 1168.

6. In contrast, Christ reassures His church, "I also will keep you *from* the hour of testing, that hour which is about to come upon the whole world, to test those who dwell on the earth" (Rev. 3:10, emphasis added).

Zephaniah's Book in Overview

Zephaniah can be divided into two broad sections, the judgment and doom section (1:2–3:8) and the joy and deliverance section (3:9–20).

Judgment and Doom (1:2–3:8)

The judgment and doom section contains prophecies against Judah, followed by prophecies against the nations, then finally prophecies against Jerusalem. Splitting these judgments like a ray of sunlight between angry thunderheads is the prophet's invitation to be saved (2:3).

Divine judgment on Judah (1:2–18). In Zephaniah's day, an attitude of arrogance and invincibility breezed across Judah like the sea air across the *Titanic's* decks. Disaster was the furthest thing from everyone's mind. A good king was on the throne; the nation was growing; the Assyrians were no longer a threat. Besides, Judah had the temple. God wouldn't destroy His temple, would He?

Zephaniah pierced their complacency with a shocking, doomsday message: "'I will completely remove all things From the face of the earth,' declares the Lord" (1:2). This was no hysterical, "sky-is-falling" threat. The same God who created the world with a word could destroy it if He wanted to—and He will, in the future judgment day (see 2 Pet. 3:7–13). Against this grim, apocalyptic backdrop, Zephaniah set the scene for Judah's fast-approaching day of reckoning.

God would stretch out His hand against five groups of Jews: idolaters (Zeph. 1:4–6), worldly princes (vv. 7–8), violent oppressors (v. 9), corrupt merchants (vv. 10–11), and the indifferent (vv. 12–13).[7]

Of this last group—which seems to represent the root problem—Zephaniah uses the vivid description "stagnant in spirit" (v. 12). This phrase is a wine maker's expression; rendered literally, they are "thickening on their lees" (NASB margin). "Lees" is the sediment that accumulates during fermentation, fixing a wine's color and body. If it is not poured off, the wine becomes thick and syrupy. "'To settle upon one's lees' [is] a proverb for sloth, indifference and

---

7. John D. Hannah, "Zephaniah," in *The Bible Knowledge Commentary*, Old Testament edition, ed. John F. Walvoord and Roy B. Zuck (Wheaton, Ill.: Scripture Press Publications, Victor Books, 1985), pp. 1526–27.

the muddy mind."[8] In essence, as the preceding verses illustrate, the people's stagnant spirits had made them sluggish in responding to God. And they had become cynical instead of faithful, saying, "'The Lord will not do good or evil!'" (v. 12b).

However, God *would* act—sooner than they thought.

> Near is the great day of the Lord,
> Near and coming very quickly;
> Listen, the day of the Lord!
> In it the warrior cries out bitterly.
> A day of wrath is that day,
> A day of trouble and distress,
> A day of destruction and desolation,
> A day of darkness and gloom
> A day of clouds and thick darkness.
> (vv. 14–15; see also vv. 16–18)

Invitation (2:1–3). "Gather yourselves together, yes, gather," Zephaniah pleaded with his people (v. 1), "Before the day of the Lord's anger comes upon you" (v. 2). "Seek the Lord," he urged, "Seek righteousness, seek humility" (v. 3). God's sheltering mercy was available to all who would repent and come after Him.

Zephaniah then turned his attention to the surrounding nations, for soon it would be too late for them as well.

Sure doom of the nations (2:4–15). Like the four points on a compass, Zephaniah's prophecies extend from Judah in four directions: Philistia to the west (vv. 4–7), Moab and Ammon to the east (vv. 8–11), Ethiopia to the south (v. 12), and mighty Assyria to the north (vv. 13–15). For their arrogance, idolatry, and hostility toward His people, God would rain down on them desolation and destruction.

Sure doom of Jerusalem (3:1–7). Would God judge His own people any less harshly for the same sins? The answer was no. Zephaniah next zeroed in on Jerusalem and cut to the heart of the city's spiritual problems:

> Woe to her who is rebellious and defiled,
> The tyrannical city!

---

8. George Adam Smith, *The Book of the Twelve Prophets*, 2 volumes in 1, The Expositor's Bible series, ed. W. Robertson Nicoll (New York, N.Y.: A. C. Armstrong and Son, 1903), vol. 2, p. 52.

She heeded no voice,
She accepted no instruction.
She did not trust in the Lord,
She did not draw near to her God. (3:1–2)

More than anyone else, Jerusalem's greatest enemy was herself. Her rulers ravaged the people for their own gain (v. 3). Her prophets and priests cut the people off from God through their corruption (v. 4). God's justice, in contrast, was brought to light "every morning"—"He does not fail" (v. 5). But He was astounded at their hardness of heart; His judgments on the unjust nations surrounding them hadn't made a dent in their stubborn spirits. Rather, "they were eager to corrupt all their deeds" (vv. 6–8).

Jerusalem had crumbled internally, long before Babylon ripped through her towers and demolished her gates. Her rebellious attitude ate away her soul, destroying trust in God and undermining worship. For this, she would be judged.

Joy and Deliverance (3:9–20)

Although the book of Zephaniah rumbles with judgment and doom, thankfully, it culminates with joy and deliverance (3:9–20). This is the final chapter of the "day of the Lord," the light at the end of God's tunnel of judgment. Notice the blessings awaiting the faithful remnant in His kingdom:

- purity of worship (v. 9a)

- universal commitment to God (v. 9b)

- worldwide unity (v. 10)

- no more shame (v. 11)

- gentle humility (v. 12)

- no more sin (v. 13)

- heartfelt joy (v. 14)

- no more divine judgment or earthly enemies (v. 15a)

- the Lord's personal presence as the King of Israel (v. 15b)

- no more fear (v. 16)

- exaltation of the grieved, lame, and outcast (vv. 18–19)

- regathering of Jews to their land (v. 20a)

- restoration of their fortune (v. 20b)

Through Zephaniah, God gives us a glimpse into the millennial kingdom, the time when the Messiah will rule the earth in perfect peace and righteousness. When, as one great body, the redeemed will lift their voices to God in praise and adoration. When judgment and heartache will be a distant memory. When love and joy will rule the day.

> "The Lord your God is with you,
>   he is mighty to save.
> He will take great delight in you,
>   he will quiet you with his love,
>   he will rejoice over you with singing."
> (v. 17 NIV)

 Living Insights

Has a Zephaniah ever tried to warn you about a disastrous course you were taking? Did you listen? Or were you resistant—preferring to deny the iceberg ahead?

_____

_____

_____

What were the results?

_____

_____

_____

What do the following verses tell you about heeding warnings?

Proverbs 12:15 _____

Proverbs 13:18 _____

Proverbs 15:32 _____

Proverbs 19:20 _____

Ezekiel 33:1–5 _____

Has someone been sending you warning signals lately? If so, what about?

_____

_____

_____

Perhaps it's time to stop ignoring this person and listen. How tragic it would be if, years from now, someone stumbled across the following verse in the little book of Zephaniah:

> She heeded no voice,
> She accepted no instruction.
> She did not trust in the Lord,
> She did not draw near to her God. (3:2)

And thought of you.

Chapter 10

HAGGAI: PERSUASIVE PROPHET OF PRIORITIES

A Survey of Haggai

W hen we come to the prophet Haggai, we enter a new era in the history of God's people. Gone were the prophets who called out to Israel and Judah to repent and turn to the Lord. Because gone was Israel, scattered like so much chaff in the wind. Gone was Judah, her wings clipped, her spirit caged by her Babylonian captors.

> O God, why have You rejected us forever? . . .
> How long, O God, will the adversary revile? . . .
> Do not deliver the soul of Your turtledove to the
>   wild beast;
> Do not forget the life of Your afflicted forever.
> (Ps. 74:1, 10, 19)

The Lord, of course, could never forget His people. He had always planned to restore them to their land.

> "For thus says the Lord, 'When seventy years have been completed for Babylon, I will visit you and fulfill My good word to you, to bring you back to this place. For I know the plans that I have for you,' declares the Lord, 'plans for welfare and not for calamity to give you a future and a hope.'" (Jer. 29:10–11; see also vv. 12–14)

Just as He had promised, God overthrew Babylon and raised up a new king, Cyrus of Persia. In 538 b.c., Cyrus, by the leading of God's Spirit, encouraged the Jews to return to Jerusalem and rebuild the Lord's temple (see Ezra 1:2–3; 6:3–5). God's people were free— they could go home to Judah!

Disappointingly, only a small group returned initially, fewer than fifty thousand. But they were aflame with enthusiasm! By the time two years had passed, they had built the altar of the Lord, were offering sacrifices according to the Law, and had laid the foundation of the temple. Opposition from their enemies, though, effectively

HAGGAI

First Message:
Rebuild God's temple

Rebuke

Reflection

Divine discipline

Repentant response

"I am with you"

Second, Third and Fourth Messages:
Encouragement and hope

"Take courage!"

"I will bless you!"

"I have chosen you!"

"First day of the sixth month" (1:1)

"Twenty-fourth day of the sixth month" (1:15)

Almost a month of silence

"Twenty-first day of the seventh month" (2:1)

"Twenty-fourth day of the ninth month" (2:10)

	CHAPTER 1	CHAPTER 2
Time	Twenty-three days	Over two months
Emphasis	Practical, negative, confronting	Spiritual, positive, comforting
Scope	Present condition of Jerusalem temple	Future glory of God's house
Theme	We must put God first in order to experience His blessings.	
Key Verses	1:4–5; 2:7–9	
Christ in Haggai	Christ's presence in this temple, which was further expanded and adorned by Herod, is "the latter glory. . . . greater than the former" (2:9a). Jesus is "our peace" (Eph. 2:14). His death on the cross has made us at peace with God now, and His future rule in His glorious Kingdom will establish worldwide peace (Hag. 2:9b). The righteous leader Zerubbabel is also a type of Christ and part of Jesus' genealogy.	

90

doused their spark of eagerness. The Lord's temple remained unfinished for fifteen years (see Ezra 4–6).

In this new world of "a future and a hope," Haggai ministered to a discouraged and spiritually apathetic remnant. His prophetic prodding, though, was always backed by the reassurance that God was still with His people, as He had been from the beginning.

The Prophet Haggai

Haggai is the first postexilic prophet. His name means "festal" or "festival," and perhaps it pointed to the celebration to come when the Jews would finish building the temple (compare Ezra 6:14b–18). Some commentators believe he was born during the Babylonian captivity. Others, however, make a case for his being born before Jerusalem's destruction in 586 B.C., based on his comparison in Haggai 2:3 between the rebuilt temple and Solomon's glorious temple. If this is true, he would probably have been in his seventies when he delivered God's message to the people.

A contagious enthusiasm permeates his writing style. In the two small chapters of his book, he delivers four messages—initially rebuking, then encouraging. He often repeats key phrases to make sure his points get across: "Thus says the Lord of hosts" (Hag. 1:2, 5, 7; 2:6, 11), "Consider your ways!" (1:5, 7), "I am with you" (1:13; 2:4), and "Take courage" (three times in 2:4). His main theme is, Rebuild the temple! But threaded throughout the book is the implicit admonition to place God before all else—and keep Him there.

Haggai's Prophetic Messages

Haggai's four prophecies form four natural divisions in his book: the call to rebuild God's temple (chap. 1); the surpassing glory of the new temple (2:1–9); the once-cursed people now blessed (2:10–19); and a special promise to Zerubbabel (2:20–23).

The Call to Rebuild the Temple (Chap. 1)

With his characteristic attention to detail, Haggai tells us exactly when he delivered God's first message: "In the second year of Darius the king, on the first day of the sixth month" (Hag. 1:1a). By modern reckoning, the date would be either August 29 or September 1, 520 B.C. It was a day to remember, for no prophet had spoken since Ezekiel or Daniel.

He next tells us that he delivered his prophecy to the returnees' leaders: Zerubbabel, the governor, and Joshua (called Jeshua in Ezra), the high priest (v. 1b). Both Zerubbabel and Joshua represented continuity with the covenant community of old. Zerubbabel was David's descendant, part of God's chosen kingly line and the family through whom His Messiah would come. In fact, Zerubbabel is listed in both Matthew's and Luke's genealogies of Jesus (see Matt. 1:12; Luke 3:27). Joshua's father, Jehozadak, came from the Aaronic line of priests and served in Jerusalem when Nebuchadnezzar had exiled the land (see 1 Chron. 6:15).

By way of these leaders, Haggai proclaimed this word from the Lord to the people:

> "Thus says the Lord of hosts, 'This people says, "The time has not come, even the time for the house of the Lord to be rebuilt."' . . . Is it time for you yourselves to dwell in your paneled houses while this house lies desolate?" (Hag. 1:2, 4)

Rather than trusting God to overcome their enemies and work on their behalf for His glory, it looks like the newly-freed remnant had capitulated to their enemies' pressure. Maybe God didn't want His temple built just yet, they had decided. So for fifteen years they had concentrated on less objectionable projects—their own houses. And not just simple houses, but luxurious "paneled" dwellings.

To them Haggai exclaimed, "Consider your ways!" (v. 5). For the Lord had been holding them to the covenant curses in Deuteronomy 28 and denying them satisfaction in all they pursued. "You have sown much, but harvest little; you eat, but there is not enough to be satisfied; . . . he who earns, earns wages to put into a purse with holes. . . . You bring it home, I blow it away" (Hag. 1:6, 9–11). In case they missed the message of their own experience, the Lord made it clear why this was happening: "Because of My house which lies desolate, while each of you runs to his own house" (v. 9b).

The solution was to "'go up to the mountains, bring wood and rebuild the temple, that I may be pleased with it and be glorified,' says the Lord" (v. 8). Happily, the people listened and obeyed what God's prophet said (v. 12). So the Lord gave them tender assurance of His presence and support: "'I am with you,' declares the Lord" (v. 13). And only twenty-three days later, with the Lord stirring their hearts, Zerubbabel, Joshua, and all the remnant got themselves organized and started work on the temple again (vv. 14–15).

The Surpassing Glory of the New Temple (2:1-9)

About a month later, discouragement seeped into the community once more. Perhaps the weeds and rubble of the years of neglect proved daunting to clear away. But more than that, the inferiority of this temple compared to the splendor of Solomon's seemed to weigh everyone down (2:3). So God sent Haggai with another message.

> "'Take courage, Zerubbabel,' declares the Lord, 'take courage also, Joshua son of Jehozadak, the high priest, and all you people of the land take courage,' declares the Lord, 'and work; for I am with you,' declares the Lord of hosts." (v. 4)

Just as He was with the Israelites when He brought them out of Egypt, so He would be with them now (v. 5). "'Do not fear!'" He encouraged His people. For in a little while, He would "'shake the heavens and the earth, . . . I will shake all the nations; and they will come with the wealth of all nations, and I will fill this house with glory,' says the Lord of hosts" (vv. 6–7). The wealth of His earth is His to do with as He pleases (v. 8; compare 1 Chron. 29:11–16). And so are the nations that He would shake—and how they were shaken! After Medo-Persia overthrew Babylon, the Persians were overthrown by the Greeks; the Greek empire dissolved into four fighting factions; and ultimately Rome prevailed (see Dan. 7–8, 11).[1]

Then Haggai ended the Lord's message with this promise:

> "'The latter glory of this house will be greater than the former,' says the Lord of hosts, 'and in this place I will give peace,' declares the Lord of hosts." (Hag. 2:9)

This promise, authors Bruce Wilkinson and Kenneth Boa explain,

> points ahead to the crucial role the second temple is to have in God's redemptive plan. Herod the Great later spent a fortune on the project of enlarging and

---

1. Commentator James Montgomery Boice adds, "There are reasons to think that God was also pointing to more distant events. In the New Testament the author of Hebrews takes Haggai's words and applies them to the shaking that will take place at God's final judgment. He warns that everything that is not firmly established in the kingdom of Christ will be plucked up and blown away [see Heb. 12:26–27]. . . . In [Haggai 2:6–7] the earlier, former shakings are evidence of the greater shaking to come." *The Minor Prophets*, 2 vols. in 1 (Grand Rapids, Mich.: Kregel Publications, 1986), vol. 2, p. 149.

enriching this temple, and it was filled with the glory of God incarnate every time Christ came to Jerusalem.[2]

The Blessing of the Once-Cursed People (2:10–19)

Two more months went by before the Lord gave Haggai another message to deliver. He was to ask the priests if holiness could be transmitted by touching something consecrated (vv. 11–12). The answer was no. Then he asked whether something could be defiled through mere contact, and the answer was yes (v. 13). The lesson was that holiness cannot be transferred, but contamination pollutes everything. "'So is this people,'" the Lord declared (v. 14). James Montgomery Boice illuminates this difficult passage.

> God explains that it has been like that with Israel. They have been living in a contaminated state due to their inverted priorities, and, as a result, everything they have touched has been contaminated. . . . But now they have turned to God, and therefore from this point on the situation will be different.[3]

"Consider from this day onward," Haggai urges three times (vv. 15, 18), how the disobedience of putting themselves before God had brought the covenant curses (see vv. 15–19a). But when they repented and obeyed the Lord's command, He graciously promised, "'From this day on I will bless you'" (v. 19b).

A Promise to Zerubbabel (2:20–23)

Later that same day, a scant four months since he began his prophetic ministry, Haggai received his last word from the Lord. The recipient this time was Zerubbabel alone, perhaps because he, as the remnant's leader, needed fresh courage for the task at hand. Haggai told him that once again the heavens and earth would be shaken; and thrones and kingdoms, chariots, horses, and riders would all topple before the Lord (vv. 21–22). But God had a reassuring plan He wanted Zerubbabel to know about.

"'On that day,' declares the Lord of hosts, 'I will take

---

2. Bruce Wilkinson and Kenneth Boa, *Talk Thru the Old Testament*, vol. 1 of *Talk Thru the Bible* (Nashville, Tenn.: Thomas Nelson Publishers, 1983), pp. 284–85.

3. Boice, *The Minor Prophets*, p. 151.

you, Zerubbabel, son of Shealtiel, My servant,'
declares the Lord, 'and I will make you like a signet
ring, for I have chosen you,'" declares the Lord of
hosts. (v. 23)

As the Lord's signet ring, he was not only safe on God's hand,
but he was the seal of God's promise to provide a future Messiah
from David's line. Now that's a future and a hope!

"I am with you" . . . "In this place I will give peace" . . .
"From this day on I will bless you" . . . "I have chosen you." These
are the concluding messages from Haggai's four prophecies to the
tiny remnant in Judah. But they remain available for anyone today
who would put their priorities in order and keep God first.

 Living Insights

Does obedience really matter so much in this New Testament
era of grace? After all, we're not under the Law or bound by the
old covenant. But . . . didn't Jesus lay out some terms for us?

> "Seek first His kingdom and His righteousness, and
> all these things will be added to you." (Matt. 6:33)

> "You are My friends if you do what I command you."
> (John 15:14)

> "If you keep My commandments, you will abide in
> My love." (John 15:10a; see also 14:21)

It looks like obediently putting God first is here to stay!

We may not receive the old blessings and curses the way Haggai's
generation did. But our fellowship with the Lord is definitely affected by our priorities.

Choose Him first, won't you? Let's be a community that longs
to hear Him say, "I am with you." There's nothing in this life that
can compare to drawing close to the eternal heart of God.

Chapter 11

ZECHARIAH:
MAN OF VISION AND FAITH
A Survey of Zechariah

The Lord remembers."

That's what Zechariah means. It's a name reminiscent of God's covenant faithfulness to His people. A name shared by about thirty different men in Scripture. A name befitting our next minor prophet.

Zechariah's prophecy resonates with God's faithful remembrance of the Jews—bright promises of a restored temple, a blessed Savior, and a future glorious age when the Lord will vanquish all His foes and usher in unprecedented blessing for those who trust in Him.

Ever wonder if God has forgotten you? If He will indeed be there waiting for you when this life is over? If history's final chapter will end happily for those who have put their faith in Christ? Then Zechariah has a promise for you: "The Lord remembers."

Historical Background

Zechariah, son of Berechiah and grandson of Iddo, came from a priestly line (see Neh. 12:4). Born in Babylonian captivity, he returned to Jerusalem under Cyrus' decree with his grandfather and about fifty thousand other exiles in 538 B.C. Zechariah was a contemporary of Zerubbabel the governor of Judah, Joshua the high priest, and Haggai the prophet.

In the late autumn of 520 B.C., just two months after Haggai began exhorting the returned exiles to restart construction of the temple, the young Zechariah began his ministry in Jerusalem. Like Haggai, Zechariah urged the people to complete the temple. But his message varied in emphasis from Haggai's.

Comparison of Zechariah and Haggai

Zechariah's prophecy (fourteen chapters) is much longer than Haggai's (two chapters). Zechariah is the "'major Minor Prophet' —the longest of the Minor Prophets and second only to Isaiah

ZECHARIAH

	Call to Repentance	Encouragement and Motivation	Questions	Encouragement and Hope
		Visions		**Predictions**
		Horses and riders	Fasting	**First "Oracle":**
		Horns and craftsmen	Failure	Rejection of Messiah
		Surveyor and measuring line	Future of Zion	Preservation of Israel
		Joshua (the priest) and Satan		Deception of false prophets
		Lampstand and seven lights		
		Flying scroll and warning		**Second "Oracle":**
		Woman and a basket		Israel's final victory
		Chariots and judgment		Messiah's final victory
	CHAPTER 1:1–6	*CHAPTERS 1:7–6:15*	*CHAPTERS 7–8*	*CHAPTERS 9–14*
Time	Written during the building of the temple			Written after completion of the temple
Purpose	To motivate those working on the temple to continue in spite of their own crop failures and financial distress. Rather than rebuking or condemning, Zechariah inspired the people to work.			To give the workers hope that there was a better day, a far more glorious day yet to come. Vivid scenes of Messiah are included. He is revealed as coming, rejected, returning, and conquering.
Theme	Build the temple; build your future			
Key Verses	4:6; 8:3; 9:9–10			
Christ in Zechariah	Zechariah is second only to Isaiah in its number of Messianic passages. Among Zechariah's explicit references to Christ are the angel of the Lord (3:1–2); the righteous Branch (3:8; 6:12–13); the King-Priest (6:13); the corner-stone, tent peg, and bow of battle (10:4); the good shepherd who is sold for thirty pieces of silver (11:4–13); the pierced One (12:10), and the coming Judge and righteous King (14).			

among the prophets in messianic passages."[1]

Zechariah elaborates on what Haggai introduced, spending much more time and detail on the future of God's people and the earthly reign of the Messiah. While Haggai's dominant message could be summarized as "Build the temple!" Zechariah's theme might be summed up as "Build the temple, and so build your future!"

Both prophets, though, were interested in the spiritual renewal of the people and urged them to put God above all else.

Literary Features and Structure

Zechariah's book is primarily

> a mix of exhortation (call to repentance, 1:2–6), prophetic visions (1:7–6:8) and judgment and salvation oracles (chs. 9–14). The prophetic visions of 1:7–6:8 are called apocalyptic (revelatory) literature, which is essentially a literature of encouragement to God's people. When the apocalyptic section is read along with the salvation (or deliverance) oracles in chs. 9–14, it becomes obvious that the dominant emphasis of the book is encouragement because of the glorious future that awaits the people of God.[2]

In addition to the above sections, chapters 7–8 contain four messages that address true spirituality versus ritualistic fasting in the life of the returned Jews.

Like Daniel, Ezekiel, Revelation, and other apocalyptic books, Zechariah is swirling with enigmatic images. Many of these symbols are arranged in a mosaic style instead of in a linear, chronological fashion. But don't let that intimidate you. All these images represent encouraging, practical truths. To study Zechariah is to know the Lord. The Lord who remembers us.

Call to Repentance (1:1–6)

The prophet begins, not by predicting the future, but by reflecting on the past: "The Lord was very angry with your fathers" (1:2).

1. Bruce Wilkinson and Kenneth Boa, *Talk Thru the Old Testament*, vol. 1 of *Talk Thru the Bible* (Nashville, Tenn.: Thomas Nelson Publishers, 1983), p. 290.

2. Kenneth L. Barker and Larry L. Walker, introduction to Zechariah, in *The NIV Study Bible*, ed. Kenneth L. Barker and others (Grand Rapids, Mich.: Zondervan Bible Publishers, 1985), p. 1406.

Returning to the Promised Land and rebuilding the temple didn't guarantee God's blessing. The returnees' ancestors, after all, had the land, the temple, and so much more. Yet they disobeyed God's Law and fell under His judgment of exile. "Don't make the same mistake," God says through Zechariah. "Return to Me, and I will return to you" (v. 3).

Encouragement and Motivation (1:7–6:15)

About three months after cautioning the people about their sinful heritage, Zechariah comforts them with eight visions of their glorious future. As stone is laid upon stone to build the new temple, vision is laid upon vision to build encouragement about Israel's security in the Lord. Throughout the visions, an interpreting angel accompanies Zechariah to help him understand their meaning.

First Vision: Horses and Riders (1:7–17)

At the time of the first vision, temple reconstruction had been in progress for five months, and Haggai had already delivered his fourth and final message to the people.

In this vision, a rider on a red horse, identified as "the angel of the Lord" (vv. 11–12), explains that he and three other horsemen have conducted a reconnaissance mission throughout the earth and found it to be "peaceful and quiet" (v. 11).

Distressed by the nations' relative ease while the people of God still live under Persian domination, the angel of the Lord asks,

> "O Lord of hosts, how long will You have no com-
> passion for Jerusalem and the cities of Judah, with
> which You have been indignant these seventy
> years?" (v. 12)

God answers that He is angry with the nations for going beyond what He had intended for His people's punishment ("further[ing] the disaster," v. 15). As for the Jews, the Lord will once again raise the temple, rebuild Jerusalem, and bless those who belong to Him (vv. 16–17).

Second Vision: Horns and Craftsmen (1:18–21)

Zechariah next sees four horns, possibly of a ram or goat, which symbolize the Gentile nations that have "scattered" Israel—most likely Assyria, Egypt, Babylon, and Medo-Persia. These horns are "throw[n] down" (v. 21) by four craftsmen—nations God has raised up to judge Israel's oppressors.

Third Vision: Man with a Measuring Line (Chap. 2)

As sure as judgment will come to the nations, blessing will come to Jerusalem. It will be a city "without walls" (2:4), overflowing the boundaries marked off by the mysterious surveyor (v. 1). Jerusalem will need

> no fortification or protection because of God's presence (cf. v. 5; Ezek. 38:11). . . . The Lord will be Jerusalem's protection without and glory within (cf. Isa. 60:19). This promise looks forward to the Lord's personal presence through the Messiah in the millennial kingdom on earth.[3]

The concluding verses of chapter 2 seem to mingle Zechariah's present day and the distant future. The exiles still in Babylon are urged to come back to Jerusalem (vv. 6–7). In doing so, they will escape God's judgment of "Babylon"—the unbelieving nations— which will transpire in full force during the millennial reign of Christ (vv. 8–9). The nations will have to pay for touching "the apple of His eye" (v. 8b). During that time, God will physically live among His people in Jerusalem (vv. 10–13).

Fourth Vision: Joshua's Garments (Chap. 3)

Zechariah's visionary journey next takes him from millennial Jerusalem back to the courts of the temple. Here he witnesses what may be one of Scripture's clearest portrayals of God's gracious gift of salvation.

The high priest, Joshua, who returned from Babylon with Zechariah, stands in filthy garments before an angel of the Lord. Satan, who tries to disqualify Joshua for his unworthiness, is rebuked by the Lord (vv. 1–2). "Is this [man] not a brand plucked from the fire?" the Lord says to Satan, indicating that Joshua, representative of all Israel, has been "plucked" from judgment for a purpose.

The Lord Himself removes Joshua's soiled clothes and replaces them with clean garments (vv. 3–5), symbolizing God's forgiveness of Israel's—and our—sin. When we put our trust in Christ, God

---

3. F. Duane Lindsey, "Zechariah," in *The Bible Knowledge Commentary*, Old Testament edition, ed. John F. Walvoord and Roy B. Zuck (Wheaton, Ill.: Scripture Press Publications, Victor Books, 1985), p. 1553.

removes the filth of our sin and clothes us in His Son's perfect righteousness. Though we are indeed unworthy to stand before God, as Satan accuses, God's gracious gift allows us not only to stand before Him but to serve Him.

Forgiveness, though, comes with responsibility. As Joshua is expected to follow the Lord's commands and lead by example (vv. 6–7), so we are to live out our faith by obeying our heavenly Father.

Lest Joshua miss the symbolism, God explains that he and his priestly companions are symbols of the coming Messiah—the Branch and the Stone (vv. 8–10).

Fifth Vision: Golden Lampstand and Olive Trees (Chap. 4)

Just as the previous vision was a message of encouragement to Joshua, the high priest, this vision is intended to encourage Zerubbabel, Judah's governor.

> Then he said to me, "This is the word of the Lord
> to Zerubbabel saying, 'Not by might nor by power,
> but by My Spirit,' says the Lord of hosts." (v. 6)

Empowered by the Holy Spirit (oil in the lamps), Zerubbabel would work (plumb line) through all obstacles (mountain) to complete the temple of the Lord, helping Israel to be a light to the nations (lampstand). The two olive branches probably signify Zerubbabel and Joshua, the key civil and religious leaders of the day, who also depict the priestly and kingly roles of the Messiah.

Sixth Vision: Flying Scroll (5:1–4)

If Israel is to become a light to the nations, she must first be purged of sin. A flying scroll, thirty feet long and fifteen feet wide, symbolizes God's purifying judgment on those who break His written Law.

Seventh Vision: Woman in a Basket (5:5–11)

Zechariah's next vision continues the theme of judgment. Israel's sinfulness, symbolized by the woman in the basket, will be removed and carried away to Shinar (Babylon), a nation characterized by godlessness. "Babylonia, a land of idolatry, was an appropriate locale for wickedness—but not Israel, where God chose to dwell with his people. Only after purging it of its evil would the promised land truly be the 'holy land' (2:12)."[4]

---

4. Barker and Walker, footnote on Zechariah 5:11, in The NIV Study Bible, p. 1412.

Eighth Vision: Four Chariots (6:1–8)

In a vision similar to the first, Zechariah now sees four chariots drawn by horses of varied colors. These "four spirits of heaven" blanket the four corners of the earth, dispensing judgment on the nations.[5]

The Crowning of Joshua (6:11–15)

Though technically not a vision, this passage serves as a symbolic climax to the previous eight visions. The Lord instructs Zechariah to place a crown upon the head of Joshua, the high priest—an event that looks forward to the Messiah who will come as the Priest-King to sit on David's throne.

True Spirituality (Chaps. 7–8)

Chapters 1–6 promise the remnant a secure future in the Lord. But what about their present? What about the returned exiles who have established a pattern of living in Babylon but want to honor God in this new phase of life? Author James Montgomery Boice transitions us into this next section.

> [The] matter of religious indifference fills the middle portion (chapters 7 and 8) of the Book of Zechariah. By the time these words were written, approximately two years had passed since the prophet had received the visions of chapters 1–6. The temple was now halfway to completion. Seeing this, a delegation from the outlying town of Bethel had come to Jerusalem to ask the priests and prophets whether it was proper for them to continue a fast marking the destruction of the temple that they and their fathers had been observing since the fall of Jerusalem seventy years before.[6]

God's answer probes beyond the question of ceremonial protocol to the deeper issue of devotion to Him. Through Zechariah, God first indicts the Jews for drifting away from true godliness into mere formalism (7:4–7). Next, using their forefathers as a negative

---

5. Judgment in the "north" probably symbolizes Babylon, which in turn represents all nations that despise God.

6. James Montgomery Boice, *The Minor Prophets*, 2 vols. in 1 (Grand Rapids, Mich.: Kregel Publications, 1986), vol. 2, p. 183.

example, He encourages His people to "dispense true justice and practice kindness and compassion" (7:8–14; compare Isa. 58; Hos. 6:6; 12:6; Mic. 6:8). As a positive example of true religion, the Lord points to the future age of blessing and righteousness for Jerusalem (Zech. 8:1–17). Finally, God reveals that He will turn their fasts into feasts, pointing to the joy all people will experience as they worship the Lord together in the future age of blessing (vv. 18–23).

Encouragement and Hope (Chaps. 9–14)

Having foretold a future age when all nations will come together to worship the true God (8:23), Zechariah's prophecy now turns to the One who broke down the barrier between Jew and Gentile, making salvation available to all people.

The last half of the book, divided into two oracles or "burdens," was probably recorded later in Zechariah's life. The first oracle (chaps. 9–11) highlights the Messiah's First Advent and His rejection by Israel. The second oracle (chaps. 12–14) focuses on the events surrounding His Second Advent and earthly rule.

The Messiah's First Advent (Chaps. 9–11)

The first eight verses of chapter 9 describe the conquest of several cites under Alexander the Great's southward sweep along the Mediterranean coastline after 333 B.C., an event yet future to Zechariah. Jerusalem, however, was divinely protected (v. 8). History shows that Alexander passed by Jerusalem several times in his campaigns and was benevolent toward the Jews. God truly preserved His beloved Jerusalem—the city to which the Messiah would come. This points to a day yet future when "no oppressor will pass over them anymore" (v. 8b).

In His First Advent, the Messiah will enter Jerusalem's gates, not on a charging white horse, but on a lowly donkey—bringing salvation, not war (v. 9).

Zechariah sees all the way to the Second Coming as well, when the Messiah's kingdom will extend to the ends of the earth (v. 10). In that day, God will destroy Israel's enemies (vv. 11–15), restore Israel to a state of blessing (9:16–10:1), be her Shepherd and Provider (vv. 2–7), and regather her to Himself (vv. 8–12).

The first three verses of chapter 11 describe devastation on the land of Judah, possibly as a result of the nation's rejection of Jesus at His First Advent. This period may have included the destruction of Jerusalem in A.D. 70.

In the latter portion of chapter 11, Zechariah is commissioned to symbolize two types of shepherds: (1) the Good Shepherd who would be rejected by His people (vv. 12–13) and (2) a wicked shepherd, possibly the Antichrist (vv. 4–11; 14–17).

The Messiah's Second Advent (Chaps. 12–14)

Jerusalem's future will not be trouble-free. During the millennial age, the city will be attacked, but God will fight on her behalf and secure peace for the Jews (12:1–9). Afterward, God will pour out His Spirit on the Jews, who will recognize their Messiah, mournfully repent of their past rejection of Him, and turn to Him in faith (vv. 10–14).

Then a "fountain" of spiritual cleansing will be opened, and Jerusalem will know the Lord (13:1). God will further purify the land by removing all the idols and false prophets (vv. 2–6).

Verses 7–9 seem to blend past and future elements. Verse 7 looks back on the crucifixion of the Lord and the scattering of the disciples. Verses 8–9 depict the preservation of a Jewish remnant who will be purified through tribulation to enter the full measure of their covenant relationship with the Lord.

Chapter 14 (vv. 1–9 and 12–15) looks back to the battle described in chapter 12. After Jerusalem's deliverance, the Lord will return in splendor and power, setting up His kingdom "over all the earth" (14:9). And Jerusalem "will no longer be a curse, for Jerusalem will dwell in security" (v. 11).

Then all the surviving nations will worship the Messiah in Jerusalem, along with the Jews (vv. 16–20). And there will no longer be "a Canaanite in the house of the Lord of hosts in that day" (v. 21). Everyone in that glorious age, all those whom the Lord has remembered, will come and worship the returned and reigning Messiah.

 Living Insights

When dealing with apocalyptic literature, we can sometimes allow the symbols to obscure the spiritual principles they represent. Having sifted through an entire book of prophetic images, scenes from the past, and glimpses into the future, take some time now to meditate on what these revelations tell us about our Lord.

What does God's complete control of time and history tell you about His ability to bear the burdens you're under right now?

_____

_____

God Himself has removed sin (filthy garments) from those who put their trust in Christ, and He has replaced it with Christ's righteousness (clean garments). What does that tell you about the security of our salvation and the way we should respond to Satan's accusations that we don't really belong to God (see Zech. 3)?

_____

_____

_____

When is religious ceremony wrong? When is it right? What is the purpose of religious forms? Did God intend them to be a means to an end or an end in themselves (see chaps. 7–8)?

_____

_____

One day, everyone who has put his or her faith in the Messiah, Jew and Gentile alike, will assemble together to worship the Lamb of God. What attitude, then, should we take today regarding the ethnic and socioeconomic makeup of our congregations?

_____

_____

Finally, upon whose memory, faithfulness, strength, and righteousness is our future based? Ours, which is flawed and sinful? Or God's, which is perfect? (You're right; it's a loaded question.)

_____

If you can only remember one thing about this chapter, remember that the Lord remembers. Forever.

Chapter 12

MALACHI: LAST CALL BEFORE SILENCE

A *Survey of Malachi*

Zechariah had prophesied about a splendid, restored temple and all the nations of the earth streaming to it. Someday the Jews would live in a powerful new kingdom, and on the throne would sit the mighty Son of David, ruling the world in justice, peace, and prosperity (Zech. 14:9–11, 16).

This glorious hope had greatly encouraged the beleaguered remnant of Israel. But, as the years passed, the glinting rays of Zechariah's vision became obscured by the drizzling, gray reality of everyday life.

By the time of Malachi, about a generation had passed since Zechariah's ministry ended. The temple, which had been finished with tremendous celebration, was now run-down and neglected because of lack of funds. The priests were corrupt and performed their duties with a dull apathy. Families were falling apart. The economy was depressed. Parasites were devouring the crops. The rich were devouring the poor.

What went wrong?

Waiting year after year for the Lord's messianic kingdom, the people had become disillusioned and doubtful. They were like passengers at a train station waiting for a train that never came. After a while, they simply gave up hope and went back to their lives. Oh, they still went through the religious motions. They made the sacrifices. They mouthed the words. In their hearts, however, they wondered whether serving God was worth it. Their faith had withered into cynicism; their love for God's Law, into callous indifference.

Malachi's mission, then, was "to light the lamp of faith in a disheartened people,"[1] reminding them that God had kept, continued to keep, and would keep His word—and so must they.

The prophet's words become a signal to all of us to not lose sight of God's promised hope. To persevere in trust. To stay alert. To keep our lamps of faith lit while waiting for the coming of the Lord.

---

1. *New Geneva Study Bible*, gen. ed. R. C. Sproul, Old Testament ed. Bruce Waltke (Nashville, Tenn.: Thomas Nelson Publishers, 1995), p. 1485.

MALACHI

	Love	Rebuke		Hope
		Against the Priests	**Against the People**	
	Unconditional	Irreverence	Intermarriage with pagans	Fire
	Almighty	Disobedience	Indifference	Healing
	Sovereign	Cynicism	Robbing God/no tithes	"Elijah"
		Hypocrisy	Blasphemy	Family
		Offense		
	CHAPTER 1:1–5	CHAPTERS 1:6–2:9	CHAPTERS 2:10–3:15	CHAPTERS 3:16–4:6
Content	Theological	Historical		Prophetical
Direction	Looking up	Looking in		Looking ahead
Theme	God cites the priest and the people with failure to keep His covenant but offers the hope of the Messiah, the messenger of the covenant who will bring justice and salvation.			
Key Verse	"'Behold, I am going to send My messenger, and he will clear the way before Me. And the Lord, whom you seek, will suddenly come to His temple; and the messenger of the covenant, in whom you delight, behold, He is coming,' says the Lord of hosts." (3:1)			
Christ in Malachi	Malachi anticipates the first and second advents of Christ, who will fulfill God's covenant with the Jews (3:1), judge sinners (3:2–5), and bring healing to those who fear the Lord (4:2).			

107

Historical Setting—The Nation and Its Wrongs

Historically, the book of Malachi fits within the book of Nehemiah. Under Nehemiah's leadership, the people had rebuilt Jerusalem's wall in 444 B.C., against incredible odds. Feeling a renewed surge of spiritual energy, they had vowed to walk in God's Law, refrain from intermarrying, keep the Sabbath, and tithe faithfully (Neh. 9:38–10:39). Then, in a grand ceremony to dedicate the wall, the priests had purified themselves and the people (12:30). With great joy they had sounded trumpets, sung songs of praise, and offered sacrifices in celebration of God's help and their renewed commitment to Him (vv. 31–43).

Unfortunately, the revival fires had dwindled to smoldering embers. About twelve years later, Nehemiah made a trip to Persia; but when he returned to Jerusalem, he was appalled by the corruption and indifference that had come over the people while he was away (13:6).

The Jews had stopped tithing, so, without financial support, many of the ministering Levites had simply gone home (vv. 4–11). Sabbath regulations were also being ignored (vv. 15–18). And the people were marrying foreigners again—to the point that in many homes the children couldn't even speak the language of the Jews (vv. 23–28)!

The nation was in worse shape than the broken-down walls Nehemiah saw when he first arrived. So, with the strong arms of a bricklayer, Nehemiah began resetting the people's stones of spiritual commitment. Around this period of backsliding and reform, Malachi stepped onto the scene.[2]

The Author and His Style

We don't know much about Malachi, except that his name means "My messenger" (compare Mal. 3:1). Some scholars think "Malachi" might be a title rather than a specific person's name. But it's equally probable that a real person by the name of Malachi did write this book, and the phrase "My messenger" in 3:1 could be a play on his name to reinforce the message of his book.

2. Because the sins Malachi confronts in his book are very similar to those Nehemiah dealt with, scholars place Malachi's book near the time of Nehemiah's reforms—either before, during, or after them.

Unlike the sermons or proclamations of the other prophets, Malachi's message comes in a question-and-answer style: God makes a statement or charge; the people challenge God with a cynical question; God drives home His point with scathing evidence. This would have been the most effective technique not only to communicate God's message but also to fully expose the people's bitter attitude. The following chart highlights God's initial statement and the people's skeptical response:

Verse	God's Statements	People's Questions
1:2	"I have loved you."	"How have You loved us?"
1:6	"'Where is My respect?' says the Lord of hosts to you, O priests who despise My name."	"How have we despised Your name?"
1:7	"You are presenting defiled food upon My altar."	"How have we defiled You?"
2:13–14	"You cover the altar of the Lord with tears . . . because He no longer regards the offering or accepts it with favor from your hand."	"For what reason?"
2:17	"You have wearied the Lord with your words."	"How have we wearied Him?"
3:7	"Return to Me, and I will return to you."	"How shall we return?"
3:8	"You are robbing Me!"	"How have we robbed You?"
3:13	"Your words have been arrogant against Me."	"What have we spoken against You?"

Christ in Malachi

A couple of messianic themes course through the book. The first is revealed in Malachi's name, "My messenger." As God's messenger, Malachi speaks specifically to the priests, who are falling down on the job as God's messengers to the people (2:7–8). Someday, however, God will send another *malachi*—whom the gospels reveal as John the Baptizer. His job will be to prepare the way for yet another messenger, the much-awaited "messenger of the covenant"—Jesus Christ, at His first coming (3:1). With these prophecies, the book of Malachi forms a vital link between the Old and the New Testaments.

The picture of Christ's second coming is even more prominent in Malachi. Like many of the Old Testament prophets, Malachi saw the mountain peaks of Christ's first and second coming as consecutive events without the gap of the church age in between. So we go from Jesus' earthly visits to the temple (3:1)—as a baby, as a young man, as the purifier of the temple, as a teacher, and as a sacrificial lamb—directly to His coming as a refining judge at the end of time (vv. 2–4). On that day, the Day of the Lord, He will judge all people, including His own. His coming will be a bane for the wicked but a boon for the righteous, who will finally receive the rewards of their faith.

One final link to Christ is the theme of God's name being great among the nations (see 1:5, 11, 14; 3:12). The Lord's wanting His name magnified "beyond the border of Israel" (1:5) foreshadows Christ's going beyond national boundaries to form a spiritual kingdom that includes Gentiles.

Survey of the Book

Malachi delivers three major messages in his book: a message of love, a message of rebuke, and a message of hope.

Message of Love

The prophet begins with God's word of reassurance, "'I have loved you,' says the Lord" (1:2a). Israel, however, does not see love but only hardship and unfulfilled promises from God. Embittered, they fire back, "'How have You loved us?'" (v. 2b).

God's love has gilded every page of their history. How can they not see it? Commentator Peter C. Craigie explains:

> Just as children from time to time may claim that they are not loved, in the face of a lifetime of parental love, so too did Israel. It had come to take for granted every sign of love, and thus ignored the signs, but the least little hardship or difficulty loomed as evidence of an unloving God.[3]

3. Peter C. Craigie, Twelve Prophets, The Daily Study Bible series (Philadelphia, Pa.: Westminster Press, 1985), vol. 2, p. 228.

110

To remind them of His love, God contrasts Jacob, whom He has chosen, with Esau, whom He has rejected.[4] God gave land and an inheritance to Jacob's offspring, but He

> "made [Esau's] mountains a desolation and appointed his inheritance for the jackals of the wilderness." (v. 3)

Instead of appreciating their blessed state as God's own chosen people, the Jews grumble about the difficulties their own sins have caused and spurn their covenant with God. For this, the Lord has a scathing rebuke.

Message of Rebuke

God first targets the priests. He accuses them of despising His name and "presenting defiled food upon My altar." Piously, they reply, "How have we despised Your name?" and "How have we defiled You?" (vv. 6–7). God answers with four charges.

- *Disobedience.* Violating the Law, they offer Him blind, lame, and sick animals (compare Lev. 22:21–22)—animals they would be embarrassed to serve an earthly ruler. It would be better to lock up the temple than to insult the King of Kings with these wretched offerings (Mal. 1:8–10).

- *Cynicism.* Ironically, these same priests reject the food offering the people bring to the Lord's table. They "disdainfully sniff at it" and say it isn't good enough (vv. 11–14).

- *Hypocrisy.* How devout the priests look as they stand in their white linen robes and pronounce their blessings. But the wicked actions beneath their religious veneer disclose hearts of contempt for God. God warns that if they don't start taking Him seriously, He will take the animal's refuse (the unclean entrails) and smear it on their faces—a startling symbol of His rejection (2:1–4).

- *Irreverence.* God had called the priests into a special covenant with Himself, the covenant with Levi (see Num. 25:10–13). Yet, instead of walking with God, they have walked away from

---

4. God uses covenant language when He says that He "loved Jacob" but "hated Esau" (vv. 2–3). Before the twins were ever born, He chose Jacob to be the one through whom He would make a nation for Himself and ultimately bring the Messiah. God, in His omniscience, also knew that Esau would be spiritually insensitive (see Gen. 25:27–34).

Him. Instead of helping others know God, they have made them stumble. Therefore, instead of honoring them, God will shame them before the people (Mal. 2:5–9).

In verse 10, God turns to the people. For they, too, have profaned the covenant. How? First, by intermarrying with pagan peoples, a clear violation of God's long-standing command (see Deut. 7:3–4); and second, by divorcing the Jewish "wife of [their] youth" (Mal. 2:11–14). Are they sorry for their unfaithfulness? No! They weep only for their lost blessings (v. 13). So God does not mince words with them—He calls their behavior treachery, saying emphatically, "I hate divorce" (v. 16). Clearly, our relationships with others are tied directly to our relationship with God (see Matt. 5:23–24). If we mistreat people, break our commitments, and use others for our selfish purposes, how can we expect God's blessing in our lives?

Malachi next tells the people that they have "wearied the Lord" with their faithless, cynical words. They have given up believing in God's covenant and character, deciding that sinners are the ones who prosper in this life. Chapter 2 ends with them sneering, "Where is the God of justice?" (v. 17).

And chapter 3 answers their question:

> "Behold, I am going to send My messenger, and he will clear the way before Me. And the Lord, whom you seek, will suddenly come to His temple; and the messenger of the covenant, in whom you delight, behold, He is coming," says the Lord of hosts. (3:1)

"Where is the God of justice you have given up on?" It's as if the Lord asks the question rhetorically, defining their doubts. Then He answers, in effect, "He is coming—with a justice that will address *your* sins" (see vv. 2–5). They will pass through God's purifying fire "so that they may present to the Lord offerings in righteousness" (v. 3).

Because of His unchanging mercy (v. 6), God offers them a second chance: "'Return to Me, and I will return to you,' says the Lord of hosts." But again they respond, "'How shall we return?'" (v. 7). So God again spells it out for them. The answer is to stop shortchanging God and give the tithes they pledged (vv. 8–10). By offering their firstfruits, they will demonstrate their commitment to worship and their trust in God to provide for their needs. In return, He promises to get rid of the "devourer" (the parasites) and bless their harvests (vv. 11–12). "'Test Me now in this'" the Lord urges (v. 10).

Sadly, they can't get their envious eyes off their successful pagan neighbors long enough to trust Him. "'It is vain to serve God,'" they bitterly complain. "'What profit is it that we have kept His charge, and that we have walked in mourning before the Lord of hosts?'" (v. 14). They truly believe they deserve better from God. What arrogance!

Message of Hope

God *will* give them what they deserve—judgment! However, He will spare those who fear Him and "esteem His name" (v. 16). "'They will be Mine,' says the Lord of hosts" (v. 17). On the day of the Lord, they will be separated from the wicked like grain from chaff, and the chaff will be set ablaze (3:18–4:1). Then the full blessings of God will rain down on them.

> "For you who fear My name, the sun of righteousness will rise with healing in its wings; and you will go forth and skip about like calves from the stall. You will tread down the wicked, for they will be ashes under the soles of your feet on the day which I am preparing," says the Lord of hosts. (4:2–3)

He then exhorts them to stay faithful to the law of Moses (v. 4), for,

> "Behold, I am going to send you Elijah the prophet before the coming of the great and terrible day of the Lord. He will restore the hearts of the fathers to their children and the hearts of the children to their fathers, so that I will not come and smite the land with a curse." (vv. 5–6)

With these words, the book of Malachi and the Old Testament come to an end. But the drama is far from over. Like a good story-teller, God leaves us on the edge of our seats, waiting for the resolution of the plot: His climactic rescue of humanity from the curse of sin.

For now, a curtain of night falls as four hundred years of divine silence settle on the earth. Who will "Elijah the prophet" be? When will the rays of God's "sun of righteousness" break through the darkness and light up the eastern sky? And who will be there to welcome the new day?

All these questions are answered when God breaks His long silence in the Gospels, which we'll survey in the next installment of *God's Masterwork*.

 Living Insights

Curse. The final prophetic word. The end note of the Old Testament. Of all the words God could have chosen to ring in His people's ears until the time of Christ, He chose that one. Why?

Because, from the beginning—since Adam and Eve—we have been prone to turn away from God, to turn away from life to death, to turn away from God's blessing to live under sin's curse. Throughout the Old Testament—from the period of the patriarchs, to the Egyptian bondage, the wanderings, the judges, the kings, the exile, and finally to the restoration—God has pursued a people who consistently showed that they could not (or would not) live up to His holy and life-giving standards. So the curse still blackens the sky.

Just as constant as the curse, though, has been the shimmering promise of redemption. God's messianic flame has wended its way through the Old Testament, shedding glimpses of a Redeemer— the One who will bear the curse and break the grip of darkness. What do the following verses tell you about this Curse-bearer?

Isaiah 53:4–6 _____

_____

Isaiah 53:10–12 _____

_____

Isaiah 61:1–3 _____

_____

The New Testament opens with God's faithful remnant searching the night sky for messianic light. As prophesied, the flame arose, not as a candle—but as a sunrise, bathing the world in its glory.

Do you need to be reminded that, as a Christian, you're no longer living under a cloud, under the curse of shame and guilt, fear and pain? In Christ, a new day has dawned! Christ has borne

your curse. Come! Warm yourself in the light of His forgiveness
and healing.

> "But for you who fear My name, the sun of righteousness will rise with healing in its wings; and you will go forth and skip about like calves from the stall." (Mal. 4:2)

> But there will be no more gloom for her who was in anguish. . . .
> The people who walk in darkness
> Will see a great light;
> Those who live in a dark land,
> The light will shine on them. (Isa. 9:1a, 2)

BOOKS FOR PROBING FURTHER

Congratulations! With the completion of the first three volumes of *God's Masterwork*, you have surveyed the *entire* Old Testament. You've seen the world created . . . and creation corrupted. You've seen God choose a nation to be His own, deliver them, nurture them, discipline them, love them. You've watched kings fall, shepherds rise, and prophets weep. You have seen the faithfulness of God shine through the bleak unfaithfulness of humanity. But the story is not over.

Our next stop is volume 4, where Old Testament shadow and prediction come to full light and fulfillment in the New Testament— in the birth, life, death, and resurrection of Jesus Christ.

Why not use this "intertestamental" break to look more closely at how He is revealed in the Old Testament, particularly in the Minor Prophets? The following resources will enrich your study.

Benware, Paul N. *Understanding End-Times Prophecy*. Chicago, Ill.: Moody Press, 1995.

Boice, James Montgomery. *The Minor Prophets: Two Volumes Complete in One Edition*. Grand Rapids, Mich.: Kregel Publications, 1986.

Clowney, Edmund P. *The Unfolding Mystery: Discovering Christ in the Old Testament*. Colorado Springs, Colo.: NavPress, 1988.

Craigie, Peter C. *Twelve Prophets*. The Daily Study Bible Series. Volumes 1 and 2. Philadelphia, Pa.: Westminster Press, 1984, 1985.

Gaebelein, Frank E., gen. ed. *The Expositor's Bible Commentary*. Vol. 7. Grand Rapids, Mich.: Zondervan Publishing House, 1985.

Grenz, Stanley J. *The Millennial Maze: Sorting Out Evangelical Options*. Downers Grove, Ill.: InterVarsity Press, 1992.

Kidner, Derek. *The Message of Hosea: Love to the Loveless*. The Bible Speaks Today Series. Downers Grove, Ill.: InterVarsity Press, 1984.

Motyer, J. A. *The Message of Amos: The Day of the Lion*. The Bible Speaks Today Series. Downers Grove, Ill.: InterVarsity Press, 1988.

Walvoord, John F., and Roy B. Zuck, eds. *The Bible Knowledge Commentary*. Old Testament edition. Wheaton, Ill.: Scripture Press Publications, Victor Books, 1985.

Wilkinson, Bruce, and Kenneth Boa. *Talk Thru the Bible*. Nashville, Tenn.: Thomas Nelson Publishers, 1983.

Some of these books may be out of print and available only through a library. For those currently available, please contact your local Christian bookstore. Books by Charles R. Swindoll may be obtained through Insight for Living. IFL also offers some books by other authors—please note the ordering information that follows and contact the office that serves you.

ORDERING INFORMATION

GOD'S MASTERWORK
Volume Three
Cassette Tapes and Study Guide

This Bible study guide was designed to be used independently or in conjunction with the broadcast of Chuck Swindoll's taped messages which are listed below. If you would like to order cassette tapes or further copies of this study guide, please see the information given below and the order form provided at the end of this guide.

		U.S.	Canada
GM3	Study guide	$ 4.95	$ 6.50
GM3CS	Cassette series, includes all individual tapes, album cover, and one complimentary study guide	40.75	47.00
GM3 1–6	Individual cassettes, includes messages A and B	6.00	7.48

Prices are subject to change without notice.

GM3 1-A: *Hosea: Love That Never Dies*—A Survey of Hosea
       B: *Joel: Preparing for the Day of the Lord*—A Survey of Joel

GM3 2-A: *Amos: From Fig-Picker to Prophet-Preacher*—A Survey of Amos
       B: *Obadiah: Strong Warning to the Proud*—A Survey of Obadiah

GM3 3-A: *Jonah: The Prodigal Prophet*—A Survey of Jonah
       B: *Micah: Advocate for the Poor*—A Survey of Micah

GM3 4-A: *Nahum: The Consequences of Negligence*—A Survey of Nahum
       B: *Habakkuk: Wrestling, Waiting, Praying, Praising*—A Survey of Habakkuk

GM3 5-A: *Zephaniah: Bright Light in a Dark Day*—A Survey of Zephaniah
       B: *Haggai: Persuasive Prophet of Priorities*—A Survey of Haggai

GM3   6-A: *Zechariah: Man of Vision and Faith*—A Survey of
Zechariah
   B: *Malachi: Last Call before Silence*—A Survey of Malachi

HOW TO ORDER BY PHONE OR FAX
(Credit card orders only)

Web site: http://www.insight.org

United States: 1-800-772-8888 or FAX (714) 575-5684, 24 hours a day,
7 days a week

Canada: 1-800-663-7639 or FAX (604) 532-7173, 24 hours a day, 7 days
a week

Australia and the South Pacific: (03) 9877-4277 from 8:00 A.M. to
5:00 P.M., Monday through Friday.
FAX (03) 9877-4077 anytime, day or night

Other International Locations: call the International Ordering Services
Department in the United States at (714) 575-5000 from 8:00 A.M.
to 4:30 P.M., Pacific time, Monday through Friday
FAX (714) 575-5683 anytime, day or night

HOW TO ORDER BY MAIL

United States
• Mail to: Mail Center
Insight for Living
Post Office Box 69000
Anaheim, CA 92817-0900
• Sales tax: California residents add 7.75%. Texas residents add 8.25%.
• Shipping and handling charges must be added to each order. See chart
on order form for amount.
• Payment: personal checks, money orders, credit cards (Visa, MasterCard,
Discover Card, and American Express). No invoices or COD orders available.
• $10 fee for *any* returned check.

Canada
• Mail to: Insight for Living Ministries
Post Office Box 2510
Vancouver, BC V6B 3W7
• Sales tax: please add 7% GST. British Columbia residents also add 7%
sales tax (on tapes or cassette series).

- Shipping and handling charges must be added to each order. See chart on order form for amount.
- Payment: personal cheques, money orders, credit cards (Visa, Master-Card). No invoices or COD orders available.
- Delivery: approximately four weeks.

Australia and the South Pacific
- Mail to: Insight for Living, Inc.
     GPO Box 2823 EE
     Melbourne, Victoria 3001, Australia
- Shipping: add 25% to the total order.
- Delivery: approximately four to six weeks.
- Payment: personal checks payable in Australian funds, international money orders, or credit cards (Visa, MasterCard, and Bankcard).

United Kingdom and Europe
- Mail to: Insight for Living
     c/o Trans World Radio
     Post Office Box 1020
     Bristol BS99 1XS
     England, United Kingdom
- Shipping: add 25% to the total order.
- Delivery: approximately four to six weeks.
- Payment: cheques payable in sterling pounds or credit cards (Visa, MasterCard, and American Express).

Other International Locations
- Mail to: International Processing Services Department
     Insight for Living
     Post Office Box 69000
     Anaheim, CA 92817-0900
- Shipping and delivery time: please see chart that follows.
- Payment: personal checks payable in U.S. funds, international money orders, or credit cards (Visa, MasterCard, and American Express).

Type of Shipping	Postage Cost	Delivery
Surface	10% of total order*	6 to 10 weeks
Airmail	25% of total order*	under 6 weeks

Use U.S. price as a base.

Our Guarantee: Your complete satisfaction is our top priority here at Insight for Living. If you're not completely satisfied with anything you order, please return it for full credit, a refund, or a replacement, as *you* prefer.

Insight for Living Catalogs: The Insight for Living catalogs feature study guides, tapes, and books by a variety of Christian authors. To obtain a free copy, call us at the numbers listed above.

Order Form
United States, Australia, and Other International Locations
(Canadian residents please use order form on reverse side.)

GM3CS represents the entire *God's Masterworks, Volume Three* series in a special album cover, while GM3 1–6 are the individual tapes included in the series. GM3 represents this study guide, should you desire to order additional copies.

Product Code	Product Description	Qty.	Price	Total
GM3	Study Guide		$ 4.95	$
GM3CS	Casette Series with study guide		40.75	
GM3-	Individual cassette		6.00	
GM3-	Individual cassette		6.00	
GM3-	Individual cassette		6.00	

Amount of Order	First Class	UPS
$ 7.50 and under	1.00	4.00
$ 7.51 to 12.50	1.50	4.25
$12.51 to 25.00	3.50	4.50
$25.01 to 35.00	4.50	4.75
$35.01 to 60.00	5.50	5.25
$60.00 to 99.99	6.50	5.75
$100.00 and over	No Charge	

Rush shipping and Fourth Class are also available. Please call for details.

Order Total

UPS ☐   First Class ☐
Shipping and handling must be added.
See chart for charges.

Subtotal

Sales Tax
California destinations—add 7.75%.
Texas destinations—add 8.25%.

Non-United States Residents
Australia and Europe: add 25%.
Other: Price +10% surface or 25% airmail.

Gift to Insight for Living
Tax-deductible in the United States.

Total Amount Due $
Please do not send cash.

Prices are subject to change without notice.

Payment by: ☐ Check or money order payable to Insight for Living or
☐ Visa   ☐ MasterCard   ☐ Discover Card   ☐ American Express   ☐ Bankcard *(In Australia)*

Number

Expiration Date   /   Signature

We cannot process your credit card purchase without your signature

Name:

Address:

City: State:

Zip Code: Country:

Telephone: (   )   –   Radio Station:

If questions arise concerning your order, we may need to contact you.

Mail this order form to the Mail Center at one of these addresses:

Insight for Living
Post Office Box 69000, Anaheim, CA 92817-0900

Insight for Living, Inc.
GPO Box 2823 EE, Melbourne, VIC 3001, Australia

Order Form
Canadian Residents
(Residents of the United States, Australia, and other international locations,
please use order form on reverse side.)

GM3CS represents the entire *God's Masterworks, Volume Three* in a special album cover, while GM3 1–6 are the individual tapes included in the series. GM3 represents this study guide, should you desire to order additional copies.

Product Code	Product Description	Qty.	Price	Total
GM3	Study Guide		$ 6.50	$
GM3CS	Casette Series with study guide		47.00	
GM3-	Individual cassette		7.48	
GM3-	Individual cassette		7.48	
GM3-	Individual cassette		7.48	
			Subtotal	
			Add 7% GST	
			British Columbia Residents *Add 7% sales tax on individual tapes or cassette series.*	
			Shipping *Shipping and Handling must be added. See chart for charges.*	
			Gift to Insight for Living Ministries *Tax-deductible in Canada.*	
			Total Amount Due $	

Amount of Order	Canada Post
Orders to $10.00	2.00
$10.01 to 30.00	3.50
$30.01 to 50.00	5.00
$50.01 to 99.99	7.00
$100 and over	No charge

Loomis Courier is also available.
Please call for details.

Please do not send cash.

Prices are subject to change without notice.

Payment by: ☐ Cheque or money order payable to Insight for Living Ministries or
☐ Visa   ☐ MasterCard

Number ⌷⌷⌷⌷⌷⌷⌷⌷⌷⌷⌷⌷⌷⌷⌷⌷

Expiration Date ⌷⌷/⌷⌷   Signature _____
We cannot process your credit card purchase without your signature.

Name: ⌷⌷⌷⌷⌷⌷⌷⌷⌷⌷⌷⌷⌷⌷⌷⌷⌷⌷⌷⌷⌷⌷

Address: ⌷⌷⌷⌷⌷⌷⌷⌷⌷⌷⌷⌷⌷⌷⌷⌷⌷⌷⌷⌷⌷⌷

City: ⌷⌷⌷⌷⌷⌷⌷⌷⌷⌷⌷⌷⌷⌷⌷   Province: ⌷⌷

Postal Code: ⌷⌷⌷⌷⌷⌷   Country: ⌷⌷⌷⌷⌷⌷⌷⌷⌷

Telephone: (⌷⌷⌷) ⌷⌷⌷–⌷⌷⌷⌷   Radio Station: ⌷⌷⌷⌷

If questions arise concerning your order, we may need to contact you.

Mail this order form to the Processing Services Department at the following address:

Insight for Living Ministries
Post Office Box 2510
Vancouver, BC, Canada V6B 3W7